Overcoming Sin

by Heath Rogers

ONESTONE

BIBLICAL RESOURCES

Published by:
One Stone Press
979 Lovers Lane
Bowling Green, KY 42103

Printed in the United States of America

ISBN 10: 0-9854-9387-9
ISBN 13: 978-0-9854938-7-5

Supplemental Materials Available:
PowerPoint slides for each lesson
Answer key
Downloadable PDF

www.onestone.com

Introduction

Sin is the transgression of the law of God (1 John 3:4, KJV). Any time we transgress God's law we have sinned. We know the Bible does not rate sins as "big" or "little." Regardless of this truth, we tend to rate sins. While most Christians are good at avoiding the "big" sins, many of us struggle with "minor" sins often dismissed as flaws or faults in our character. When challenged, some will say, "I know I need to work on that," but will continue without addressing the problem. Others will claim, "That's just the way that I am," indicating they have no intention of trying to change.

Any sin, regardless of how big or little it appears in our eyes, will separate us from God and condemn our souls to an eternal Hell (Is. 59:1-2; Rev. 21:8). God expelled Adam and Eve from the Garden of Eden for eating a piece of fruit. God takes sin seriously. If we are going to have fellowship with God, we must take sin seriously.

The original title of this series of lessons was "Overcoming Sins Embedded in Our Character." Let me explain the meaning behind this long title. When I was six years old, my family lived in a house with a huge oak tree outside my bedroom window. It looked just like the rest of the trees on the property, but there was something strange about it. This particular tree had a piece of metal "growing" out of it. I was young, but I knew metal does not grow on trees. Obviously, this piece of metal had been attached to the tree in the past. As time went on, the tree grew around it. It was not a piece of the tree, and did not belong in the tree, but it was embedded in the tree.

The same thing can be said about sin in the lives of Christians. We know it is not supposed to be there, but it is. Sadly, sin is such a part of the lives of some Christians, one could say it is "embedded" in their character just like the metal was embedded in that tree. It is there, but it does not belong. It needs to be removed.

Other brethren have written good material on the subject of sin, but this workbook is different. This study addresses how to overcome some specific sins. The first two lessons identify the nature of sin and the imperative to overcome. Each remaining lesson identifies a specific sin or avenue of temptation, exposes its danger, and notes what the Bible says about overcoming the sin.

Unless otherwise noted, all Bible quotations are taken from the New King James Version.

Table of Contents

This book is dedicated to my dad, Quintin Rogers, who for the past twenty-seven years has shown me it is possible to win a battle "one day at a time." You always tell me you are proud of me. I am proud of you, and I love you very much.

THE NATURE OF SIN

It is important to know the potential dangers of things to which we are exposed. Once, when our family considered getting a dog, we looked carefully at the different breeds of dogs. Among the things we considered was whether or not a particular breed of dog made a good pet for a family with young children. We wanted to know something about the nature of the animal before we brought it into our home.

A thing's nature is its characteristics, qualities, dispositions or tendencies – that which makes it what it is. Sin is not an abstract thought, but a real and present force in our world and our lives. It has a nature, and we would do well to understand the nature of sin and the danger sin poses to our lives and the lives of those around us.

Sin is Deceptive

The Bible warns us of the fact that sin is deceitful. "But exhort one another daily, while it is called 'Today,' lest any of you be hardened through the deceitfulness of sin" (Heb. 3:13). The word "deceitfulness" comes from the Greek word which means to give a false impression by appearance, statement, or influence. Sin is not truthful with us. Sin, by its very nature, sets out to deceive us.

Consider the deceitful nature of the first sin, recorded in Genesis 3:1-8.

1. **Sin deceived Eve by making her believe there were no consequences**. Satan told her, "You will not surely die," (v. 4). Eve was convinced by Satan there would be no consequence for eating the fruit. Salesmen give us the pitch, "Buy now, pay later." They would have us believe we can make a purchase today without having to pay for it, but we know the payment eventually comes due.

2. **Sin deceived Eve by making promises it has no intention of keeping**. Satan told Eve in eating the fruit, she would become like God, thus being an equal with God (vv. 4-5). When she ate, she found out Satan's promise was a lie. Sin makes the same kinds of promises today. People believe drugs and alcohol will provide a means of escape from reality, fornication will make one's life more fulfilling, or cheating

> Sin is not an **abstract thought**, but a **real and present force** in our world and in our lives.

and lying provide a short-cut to success. These promises are all lies. Sin promises liberty but brings bondage, promises success but brings misery, promises pleasure but brings pain, promises victory but brings failure, promises life but brings death.

3. **Sin deceived Eve by making itself attractive**. Although it was a source of death, the fruit of the tree looked good and was desirable to the eyes (v. 6). Those involved in marketing know the importance of packaging products attractively. Sin comes wrapped in an attractive package. Beer and alcohol commercials make their product look like fun. People are lured into the bed of fornication because of the lust of the eyes. Sin is pleasurable, but the pleasure is only "for a season" (Heb. 11:25). The Bible warns us against the deceitfulness of lusts (Eph. 4:22), and we need to take this warning seriously.

Sin is Enslaving

The Bible does not picture sin as a harmless object to be enjoyed without consequence, but as a cruel taskmaster, catching us in a trap and reaching its tentacles into every part of our being. Jesus says, "whoever commits sin is a slave of sin" (John 8:34). Without repentance, those in sin give themselves over to a habitual practice of sin. Sin becomes a way of life for them. The Bible pictures sin as a trap or a shackle. "His own iniquities entrap the wicked man, and he is caught in the cords of his sin" (Prov. 5:22). Peter observed that Simon was "poisoned by bitterness and bound by iniquity" (Acts 8:23).

The **binding power** of sin can be so overpowering that some fail to see they are **slaves**.

The binding power of sin can be so overpowering that some fail to see they are slaves. Peter describes the miserable state of the false teachers of his day as, "while they promise them liberty, they themselves are slaves of corruption; for by whom a person is overcome, by him also he is brought into bondage" (2 Peter 2:19). How ironic—these teachers, promising men liberty if they followed their error, were slaves of corruption.

Once our sins are forgiven, we are freed from the bondage of sin (Rom. 6:17-18, 22). Though freed from our sins, the past exposure to and involvement in sin will prove to be a constant obstacle to our efforts to live pure and holy lives. The Hebrew writer encourages us to "lay aside every weight, and the sin which so easily ensnares us, and let us run with endurance the race that is set before us" (Heb. 12:1). The word "ensnares" is translated from a Greek word which means to surround or prevent the advancement of a runner. Sin continues to be an opponent who would hinder us from advancing in our service to the Lord.

Sin is not a harmless friend. We are not to believe we can indulge in sin once and walk away from it. As one has said, "It is easier to suppress the first desire than it is to satisfy all that follow it." The nature of sin is to make us slaves.

Sin is Defiling

While one may fail to see the extent to which sin has affected them, God sees the defilement caused by sin as clearly as one would see a crimson stain on a white garment. "'Come now, and let us reason together,' says the Lord, 'Though your sins are like scarlet, they shall be as white as snow; though they are red like crimson, they shall be as wool'" (Is. 1:18).

The Hebrew word translated "scarlet" referred to a bright red dye. "This color was obtained from the eggs of the *coccus ilicis*, a small insect found on the leaves of the oak in Spain, and in the countries east of the Mediterranean. The cotton cloth was dipped in this color twice; and the word used to express it means also double-dyed, from the verb *shaanaah*, to repeat... This was a fast, or fixed color. Neither dew, nor rain, nor washing, nor long usage, would remove it. Hence, it is used to represent the fixedness and permanency of sins in the heart. No human means will wash them out. No effort of man, no external rites, no tears, no sacrifices, no prayers, are of themselves sufficient to take them away. They are deep fixed in the heart, as the scarlet color was in the web of cloth, and an almighty power is needful to remove them" (Barnes 72).

At times, man is aware of this defilement. David saw the need to be washed, cleansed, and purged of his sins that he might be "white as snow" (Ps. 51:1-2, 7). At other times, this defilement has so penetrated the heart and corrupted the mind there appears to be no hope of the sinner wanting to be cleansed (Titus 1:15-16; Heb. 3:13).

Sin is not harmless. It is pollution that stains man's soul and life, thus separating him from his God (2 Cor. 6:17-7:1; 2 Pet. 2:20-22).

Sin is Destructive

It is not within sin's nature to peacefully co-exist with God's creation. Sin is lawlessness (1 John 3:4). Being opposed to God's law and standard, sin seeks to upset God's order, causing man to live in a way that God never intended for him to live. Sin is also unrighteousness (1 John 5:17). Being opposed to righteousness and justice, sin wreaks havoc upon mankind, destroying lives, families, friendships, churches, and even entire nations (Prov. 14:34).

> God sees the **defilement** caused by sin as clearly as one would see a **crimson stain** on a white garment.

Consider the destruction caused by the first sin (Gen. 3). First, sin destroyed man's innocence (v. 7). The eyes of Adam and Eve were opened, and they knew right from wrong. Second, sin destroyed man's peace with God (v. 8). For the first time, they were afraid of being in the presence of God. Third, sin destroyed man's world (v. 17). God cursed the ground because of man's sin. Finally, sin destroyed man's life (v. 19). Man became subject to physical death because of sin (Rom. 5:12). Sin is no friend of man. Sin is destructive and deadly.

Sin is Progressive

Sin is never satisfied with a small, seemingly harmless infraction. Once it has gotten its foot in the door, sin will continue to gain ground in a man's heart. The Lord and His apostles likened sin unto leaven (Matt. 16:6, 11, Luke 12:1, 1 Cor. 5:6-8). Like leaven, sin starts out small, but its influence spreads and eventually affects everything within its reach.

The progressive nature of sin is seen among groups of people. After sin's introduction, it did not take long before "the Lord saw that the wickedness of man was great in the earth, and that every intent of the thoughts of his heart was only evil continually" (Gen. 6:5).

Without repentance, sin leads to even greater involvement in sin. In Romans 1, Paul describes the progression of sin among the Gentiles. It began by their refusal to acknowledge God, which led to idolatry (vs. 20-23)—a seemingly harmless infraction, but it led to lies, self-worship, and fornication (vs. 24-25). This state led them to pursue sexual perversions (vs. 26-27). Finally, God gave them over to a debased mind to pursue all unrighteousness (vs. 28-32). Thus, we see sin digresses in a downward spiral, getting worse and worse (2 Tim. 3:13).

The progressive nature of sin is also seen in the lives of individuals. Consider the sins committed by King David regarding Bathsheba. He lusted after Bathsheba (2 Sam. 11:2). After learning she was the wife of Uriah, he sent for her and committed the sin of adultery (vv. 3-4). Bathsheba became pregnant. David tried to cover up the sin by calling her husband home from battle. When Uriah refused to go home to his wife (v. 8), David got him drunk (v. 13). When he still refused to go home to his wife, David had him killed (vv. 14-17), and then took Bathsheba to be his own wife.

Sin, by its nature, is not a harmless, one-time experience. Once sin has lured us in, it enslaves us and continues to take us further along than we ever thought we could go.

The Bible gives us an **advantage** that Adam and Eve did not have—it tells us about the **true nature** of sin.

Conclusion

Sin is an ever-present reality in our world and our lives, but it is not a harmless choice. The Bible gives us an advantage that Adam and Eve did not have—it tells us about the true nature of sin. Sin is deceptive, enslaving, defiling, destructive, and progressive. We need to learn to appreciate the fact sin is "exceedingly sinful" (Romans 7:13).

References

Barnes, Albert. *Notes on the Old Testament, Isaiah.* 1. Grand Rapids, MI: Baker Books, 1996. 72. Print.

Questions

1. What is meant when we refer to a thing's "nature?" _____
    _____
    _____

2. What does it mean to say someone or something is deceitful? _____
    _____
    _____

3. What lie did Satan tell Eve (Gen. 3:4)? _____
    _____
    _____

4. What benefit did Satan tell Eve she would receive from eating the fruit of the tree (Gen. 3:4-5)?
    _____
    _____

5. What is the state of anyone who commits sin (John 8:34)? _____
    _____
    _____

6. Does becoming a Christian free us from the enslaving nature of sin (Heb. 12:1; Acts 8:23)?
    Why or why not? _____
    _____

7. How did Israel's sins appear unto God (Is. 1:18)? _____
    _____
    _____

8. What request did David make regarding his sins (Ps. 51:1-2, 7)? _____
    _____
    _____

9. What is sin (1 John 3:4, 5:17)? _____
    _____
    _____

10. Describe the destruction caused by man's first sin (Gen. 3). _____
    _____
    _____

11. How is sin like leaven (1 Cor. 5:6-7)? _____
    _____
    _____

12. How far had sin progressed by the time of Noah (Gen. 6:5)? _____
_____
_____

13. What sins were committed by David with regard to Bathsheba and Uriah (2 Sam. 11)?
_____
_____

True or False

1. _____ We can trust things to act contrary to their nature.

2. _____ Eve did not understand the consequences of eating the fruit of the tree in the midst of the garden (Gen. 3:3).

3. _____ Sin wants to make us its slave.

4. _____ Sin cannot place a Christian in the "bond of iniquity" (Acts 8:23).

5. _____ Man is so depraved he can never be aware of how his sin has defiled his life.

6. _____ Sin destroys man's innocence.

7. _____ Given time, evil men and deceivers will eventually get better (2 Tim. 3:13).

8. _____ David had to cover up the sin he had committed with Bathsheba.

9. _____ The wages of sin is death (Rom. 6:23).

10. _____ Sin is exceedingly sinful (Rom. 7:13).

OVERCOMING IS NECESSARY

Christians are going to sin (1 John 1:8, 10). God has made a way for Christians to receive the forgiveness of their sins and continue enjoying fellowship with Him. If we will confess our sins, God is faithful to forgive us our sins (v. 9). This is possible because Jesus is both our Advocate and the Propitiation for our sins (2:1-2). An advocate represents another in court and pleads his case. A propitiation appeases or satisfies. When we pray for the forgiveness of our sins, Jesus presents our case before God. He pleads for our forgiveness, not on the basis of our innocence, but because His own blood satisfies God's law regarding the guilt of our sins.

In spite of the fact that God has made a way for Christians to continue to receive the forgiveness of their sins, it is God's will that we strive to live a life without sin. "My little children, these things I write to you, *so that you may not sin*. And if anyone sins, we have an Advocate with the Father, Jesus Christ the righteous. And He Himself is the propitiation for our sins, and not for ours only but also for the whole world" (1 John 2:1-2, emphasis mine—HR). Notice, if we sin, we have a means of receiving the forgiveness of those sins, but the goal for us is not to sin.

Jesus has not called us out of sin to continue in sin. We are not to set our moral lives on cruise-control, nor use God's grace and forgiveness as a reason to be casual about the sin in our life. Since temptation is an ever-present reality, we must make an effort to overcome sin. The following truth should help us take sin seriously and seek to overcome it when it is in our heart and life.

God Calls Us to Be Holy

"But as He who called you is holy, you also be holy in all your conduct, because it is written, 'Be holy, for I am holy'" (1 Pet. 1:15-16). To be holy means to be pure or sinless. Holiness is the standard God has set for us. Peter tells us our conduct is not to be fashioned after our former sinful lusts, but it must be fashioned after God's holiness (vv. 13-16).

Peter gives us three good reasons to strive to live holy (sinless) lives. We must be holy in order to continue enjoying fellowship with God (vv. 15-16). We must conduct ourselves in a holy

> If we sin, we have a means of receiving the **forgiveness** of those sins, but the **goal** for us is **not to sin**.

> We must be **holy** out of consideration of the **great price** paid to make us holy.

manner because of the coming judgment (v. 17). We must be holy out of consideration of the great price paid to make us holy (vv. 18-19; 1 Cor. 6:20).

Paul told the Thessalonians, "God did not call us to uncleanness, but in holiness" (1 Thess. 4:7). God did not call us to continue to live unclean, impure, sinful lives. We must possess or control ourselves (v. 4). We must remain aware of the purity of our thoughts, motives, attitudes, desires, habits, words, and actions. God does not save us from our sin so we can continue sinning. He calls us to come out of sin and live a holy life. Holiness is the goal for our life. Living a holy life is not possible unless we confront and overcome the sin in our life.

Paul told the Corinthians, "Therefore, having these promises, beloved, let us cleanse ourselves from all filthiness of the flesh and spirit, perfecting holiness in the fear of God" (2 Cor. 7:1). While it is true the blood of Jesus washes away our sins (1 John 1:7), we are responsible for *cleansing ourselves* of the filthiness or defilement of the flesh and spirit in our lives. As John said, we must *purify ourselves* as Christ is pure and holy (1 John 3:3). We must put forth an effort to live pure, holy, sinless lives.

Christians Are Dead to Sin

Christians cannot continue in sin because, in the process of becoming a Christian, we all died to sin. "What shall we say then? Shall we continue in sin that grace may abound? Certainly not! How shall we who died to sin live any longer in it?" (Rom. 6:1-2). Theoretically, it is impossible for one who has died to sin to continue in sin.

When we became a Christian, we crucified and did away with the old man of sin (the part of us that enjoyed sinning) (Rom. 6:6). We are to consider ourselves to be dead to sin—no longer able to participate in sin (v. 11). We are not to let sin reign (go unchecked or unchallenged) in our lives (v. 12). We are not to present ourselves as willing participants in sin (v. 13). Instead, we must strive to overcome sin.

Paul told the Colossians they had died, and their life was hidden in Christ (Col. 3:3). This means their life now belonged to Christ to do His will. He went on to tell them to "put to death your members which are on the earth: fornication, uncleanness, passion, evil desire, and covetousness, which is idolatry" (v. 5). We are to consider ourselves as being unable to engage in sin.

We Are to Put Off the Old Man of Sin

In the previous illustration, we were told to put to death the old man of sin. Paul also spoke of taking him off and putting him away like an old, soiled garment and replacing him with a new man of righteousness and holiness (Eph. 4:17-24). Putting off the old man of sin means we must change our way of thinking and living once we become a Christian. Paul told the Ephesians they were to be "renewed in the spirit of your mind" (v. 23). This tells us the battle to overcome sin takes place in the heart and mind. Paul went on to mention several specific sins we must "put away" (4:25-5:17).

We must change the way we think, which will change the way we live. Once we become a Christian, we can no longer pursue the pleasures of sin (1 Pet. 4:1-3). A Christian must cease from sin. The time spent in sin before we became a Christian is more than enough time of our life to be wasted pursuing sin.

God's Grace Teaches Us to Deny Ourselves

"For the grace of God that brings salvation has appeared to all men, teaching us that, denying ungodliness and worldly lusts, we should live soberly, righteously, and godly in the present age" (Titus 2:11-12). God's grace brings salvation from sin, but this grace does not teach us to take sin lightly (Rom. 6:15). God's grace teaches us to deny or renounce ungodliness and worldly lusts. If we are not making the effort to overcome sin, we are not living the way God has taught us to live.

Self-denial is the key to overcoming sin. We must learn to tell ourselves "no" when tempted to sin. Self-denial or self-control is an important part of the life of a Christian. It is necessary in order to be a disciple of Jesus (Matt. 16:24). Self-control or temperance is a part of the fruit of the Spirit (Gal. 5:23) and one of the "Christian Graces" (2 Pet. 1:6). It is necessary in order to serve as an elder (Titus 1:8) and to win the imperishable crown (1 Cor. 9:25-27).

We Are Not to Allow Sin to Control Us

In our previous lesson, we learned sin has the power to enslave us, even after we have become a Christian. Therefore, we must continue the battle to overcome sin's grip on our lives. Paul said he would not be brought under the power of anything (1 Cor. 6:12). Other versions render this phrase as "I will not be mastered by anything" (NASV) and "I will not be enslaved by anything" (ESV).

When Cain and Abel brought offerings to the Lord, He respected Able and his offering, but He rejected Cain and his offering. This made Cain angry. The Lord responded to Cain's anger with a warning and instruction regarding sin. "If you do well, will not your countenance be lifted up? And if you do not do well,

The time spent in sin **before** we became a Christian is **more than enough** time of our life to be **wasted** pursuing sin.

sin is crouching at the door; and its desire is for you, but you must master it" (Gen. 4:7, NASV). Sin is pictured as "a wild beast crouching at the door, waiting to attack the one who opens it" (Davis 100). Sin's desire is to control us, but it is up to us whether or not we open the door to sin. There is a battle between sin and self. We must rule over sin, or sin will rule over us. The Christian who refuses to confront the sin in their life is leaving the door open to sin and allowing sin to rule over them.

God Provides Help in Times of Temptation

God has not left us alone to try to "master" sin by ourselves. He is ever present to help us overcome temptation and win our battle with sin. We are to pray for God's help in overcoming temptation (Matt. 6:13). When we are tempted to sin, God provides a way of escape. "No temptation has overtaken you except such as is common to man; but God is faithful, who will not allow you to be tempted beyond what you are able, but with the temptation will also make the way of escape, that you may be able to bear it" (1 Cor. 10:13). If God cares enough to provide a way out of temptation, the least we can do is to take this way of escape from sin. For Jesus, the way of escape was Scripture (Matt. 4:4, 7, 10). For Joseph, the way of escape was literally fleeing (Gen. 39:12).

Sin Has Temporal Consequences

Although the spiritual consequences of sin can be overcome through Christ, the temporal or physical consequences will remain. For example, one who breaks the law can be forgiven by God, but he will still have to face the punishment required by man's law. An adulterer can be forgiven by God, but his sin may destroy his marriage and family. A liar can be forgiven by God, but his reputation before man will still be tarnished.

We will reap what we sow (Gal. 6:7-8). If we fail to overcome sin, we will continue to reap the temporal consequences of those sins.

Continued Sin Results in Eternal Punishment

To willfully sin after we have received knowledge of the truth places our soul in jeopardy. We are deserving of judgment and fiery indignation at the hands of the living God (Heb. 10:26-31). This passage does not describe the faithful Christian who stumbles and succumbs to temptation. It describes the Christian who sins willfully. Are we not sinning willfully if we know we have a problem with sin in our life and refuse to address it and correct it?

Are we not **sinning willfully** if we know we have a **problem** with sin in our life and **refuse** to address it and correct it?

Paul took extreme measures to practice self-control in an effort to keep from disqualifying himself from the reward (1 Cor. 9:25-27). If an inspired apostle had to show this much concern and effort regarding himself, how much more concern should you and I have? What a terrible thing it would be to lose our reward because we refused to correct the sin in our heart and life.

Conclusion

The sin in our life is not to be dismissed, ignored, tolerated, or excused. It is not just the way we are. It is God's will that new creatures (2 Cor. 5:17) walk in newness of life (Rom. 6:4). This new life is to be characterized by purity and holiness, not by a continuance in sin. It is essential we make an effort to overcome the sin in our heart and in our life. In the lessons that follow, we will focus on ways to overcome some specific sins and avenues of temptation.

References

Davis , John. *Paradise To Prison, Studies in Genesis*. Grand Rapids, MI: Baker Book House, 1975. 100. Print.

Questions

1. What are Christians to do to receive the forgiveness of their sins (Acts 8:22; 1 John 1:9)?
    _____
    _____

2. What is the goal or standard God has set for all Christians (1 John 2:1)? _____
    _____
    _____

3. What does it mean for us to be holy as God is holy (1 Pet. 1:15-16)? _____
    _____
    _____

4. What are some reasons we are to strive to live a holy life (1 Pet. 1:15-19)? _____
    _____

5. What did Paul tell the Corinthians to do (2 Cor. 7:1)? _____
    _____
    _____

6. What did John tell all Christians to do (1 John 3:3)? _____
    _____

7. What does it mean to be dead to sin (Rom. 6:1-2, 6, 11-13)? _____
    _____
    _____

8. What is necessary for us to put off the old man of sin and put on the new man of righteousness and holiness (Eph. 4:23)? _____
    _____
    _____

9. What does God's grace teach us (Titus 2:11-12)? _____
    _____
    _____

10. What warning and instruction did God give Cain regarding sin (Gen. 4:7)? _____
    _____
    _____

11. What help does God provide when we are being tempted to sin (1 Cor. 10:13)? _____
    _____
    _____

12. Does a Christian have to suffer the temporal or physical consequences of his sin? _____
    _____
    _____

13. What truth is set forth in Galatians 6:7? _____
    _____
    _____

14. What awaits the Christian who sins willfully (Heb. 10:27)? _____
    _____
    _____

15. What attitude did Paul have regarding the sin in his life (1 Cor. 9:25-27)? _____
    _____
    _____

Fill in the Blank

1. "Your _____ I have hidden in my _____, that I might not _____ against You" (Ps. 119:11).

2. "Neither do I condemn you; go and _____ no more" (John 8:11).

3. "Therefore do not let sin _____ in your mortal body, that you should _____ it in its _____" (Rom. 6:12).

4. "And do not be _____ to this world, but be _____ by the renewing of your _____, that you may prove what is that _____ and _____ and _____ will of God" (Rom. 12:2).

5. "Awake to _____, and do not _____; for some do not have the knowledge of God. I speak this to your shame" (1 Cor. 15:34).

6. "_____ from every form of _____" (1 Thess. 5:22).

7. "For the _____ of God that brings _____ has appeared to all men, _____ us that, _____ ungodliness and worldly lusts, we should live _____, _____, and _____ in the present age" (Titus 2:11-12).

8. "But as He who called you is _____, you also be _____ in all your conduct, because it is written, 'Be _____, for I am _____'" (1 Pet. 1:15-16).

9. "My little children, these things I write to you, so that _____ _____ _____ _____. And if anyone _____, we have an Advocate with the Father, Jesus Christ the righteous" (1 John 2:1).

10. "And everyone who has this hope in Him _____ himself, just as He is ____" (1 John 3:3).

THE LUST OF THE FLESH

Temptation to sin comes through three different avenues—the lust of the flesh, the lust of the eyes, and the pride of life (1 John 2:15-17). In order for us to overcome sin, we must learn how to handle these avenues of temptation. Pride is discussed in the next lesson. This lesson will focus upon lust—specifically, the lust of the flesh.

There are five different Greek words translated as "lust," "crave," or "desire" in the New Testament (*epithumia, hedone, epipotheo, orexis,* and *pathos*). These words were neutral terms, referring to any strong desire or craving. However, the words came to be used, almost entirely, in a bad sense. In the New Testament, the word "lust" is primarily a desire for things contrary to the will of God.

Regarding the "lust of the flesh," the word "flesh" does not refer to man's physical body. "Flesh" is a word the Bible uses to identify the source of evil appetites residing within man. The flesh is the part of man that desires to serve the "law of sin" (Rom. 7:25). The "lust of the flesh" is a desire for the sinful things enjoyed by our flesh.

Overcoming the "lust of the flesh" is especially difficult because these lusts, cravings, or desires are a part of us; they come from within us. As William Barclay has aptly said, "The essence of the flesh is this. No army can invade a country from the sea unless it can obtain a bridgehead. Temptation would be powerless to affect men, unless there was some thing already in man to respond to temptation. Sin could gain no foothold in a man's mind and heart and soul and life unless there was an enemy within the gates who was willing to open the door to sin. The flesh is exactly the bridgehead through which sin invades the human personality. The flesh is like the enemy within the gates who opens the way to the enemy who is pressing in through the gates" (Barclay 21-22). Overcoming sin means overcoming the lusts of the flesh, which means we must defeat the enemy within us!

In the New Testament the word **"lust"** is primarily a **desire** for things **contrary** to the will of God.

How Fleshly Lusts War Against Our Soul

"Beloved, I beg you as sojourners and pilgrims, abstain from fleshly lusts which war against the soul" (1 Peter 2:11). This admonition from the apostle Peter must be taken seriously. Our soul is the most valuable thing we have (Matt. 16:26), and it must be defended at all costs. Fleshly lusts are our enemies because they wage a war against our eternal soul.

Sin destroys man's soul, and fleshly lusts tempt us to sin. "But each one is tempted when he is drawn away by his own desires and enticed. Then, when desire has conceived, it gives birth to sin; and sin, when it is full-grown, brings forth death" (James 1:14-15). The flesh within us has lusts or desires to sin. It wants to sin. The lusts of the flesh have an alluring power (2 Pet. 2:18). When Satan appeals to and entices the flesh, he is tempting us to sin. At that point, the battle is on to give in to the temptation and satisfy our lust or resist the temptation and deny the fulfillment of our lust.

Some specific sins produced by lust are:

1. **Drunkenness and revelries** (Rom. 13:13; 1 Pet. 4:2-4). For some, the pursuit of particular lusts leads to consuming alcohol. Consumption of alcohol leads to drunkenness, drinking parties, fights, regrets, etc. People turn to drugs and alcohol for various reasons, but it is a lust or desire for the high or escape from reality causing them to continue using drugs and alcohol.

2. **Fornication.** "For this is the will of God, your sanctification: that you should abstain from sexual immorality; that each of you should know how to possess his own vessel in sanctification and honor, not in passion of lust, like the Gentiles who do not know God" (1 Thess. 4:3-5). Pursuing the "passion of lust" will result in fornication. There are some obvious things that excite the lust for sexual sins.

Dancing, by its nature, supplies an effective avenue through which individuals are tempted to pursue sexual sins. Some verses in the New Testament closely connect the words "lewdness" (lasciviousness) and "lust" (Rom. 13:13; 1 Pet. 4:3; 2 Pet. 2:18). Lewdness is translated from the Greek word *aselgeia* which means "wanton acts or manners, as filthy words, indecent bodily movements, unchaste handling of males and females" (Thayer 79-80). This is a perfect description of modern popular dancing.

Dancing excites the flesh and invites sexual sin. While some Christians try to deny this, those in the world willingly admit it. "The whole range of modern dances are designed

aselgeia:

wanton acts or manners, as filthy words, indecent bodily movements, unchaste handling of males and females to express love making" (Sach). Those in the dancing and the medical profession state that dancing is a means of stimulating sexual impulses. Much of what passes for dancing today is simply a gateway to intercourse. Why do high school dances have to be chaperoned? Why do young people reserve hotel rooms on prom night? The stimulation felt on the dance floor is no different from the stimulation felt in the bedroom.

Pornography certainly supplies an avenue of temptations for individuals to pursue sexual sins. Pornography is not innocent fantasy or a victimless crime. Jesus says the man who looks upon a woman to lust for her has already committed adultery with her in his heart (Matt. 5:28). The whole purpose for pornography is for a man to look and lust. Looking upon naked bodies, either in person or in pictures or videos, excites the flesh and invites sexual sin (2 Sam. 11:2-4).

Pornography is addictive. The sight of naked bodies sends a rush throughout the viewer's body he wants to enjoy again and again. The sinful images will be burned upon his mind and will poison his heart (Matt. 5:8). Like Job, we need to make a covenant with our eyes not to look upon a woman to lust after her (Job 31:1).

Pornography can also destroy one's marriage. While viewing pornography does not satisfy the exemption granted by Jesus in Matthew 19:9 (fornication is a physical act committed with our body, 1 Cor. 6:15-18), wives who have discovered their husbands viewing pornography feel as if their husbands have been cheating on them. The violation of trust and feelings of inadequacy ("Why am I not enough for my husband?") caused by pornography often create a great hurdle in the marriage relationship.

Immodest dress. Some parts of the body, when revealed or enhanced by certain types of clothing, excite the flesh and invite sexual sin. The Bible acknowledges the attire of a harlot, which entices men (Prov. 7:10). Much clothing worn today is designed to attract and invite sexual attention. Those who wear such clothing, either purposely or innocently, are placing a stumbling block before others (Matt. 18:6-7).

Mixed swimming excites the lust of the flesh with regard to sexual sin in two ways. First, the clothing is immodest (even the most "modest" modern one-piece swimsuits conceal very little of a woman's body). Second, swimming provides a means for contact between the bodies of individuals, further exciting the lust of the flesh. Any young person who

> Like Job, we need to make a **covenant** with our **eyes** not to look upon a woman to lust after her.

While many in our society want us to **believe** homosexuality is a **genetic disposition**, the Bible states it is the result of an **unrestrained pursuit** of vile passions and burning lusts.

claims they never had to struggle with sexual impulses while visiting a public swimming pool or water park is either lying or needs to have their eyes checked.

3. **Homosexuality.** "For this reason God gave them up to vile passions. For even their women exchanged the natural use for what is against nature. Likewise also the men, leaving the natural use of the woman, burned in their lust for one another, men with men committing what is shameful, and receiving in themselves the penalty of their error which was due" (Rom. 1:26-27). While many in our society want us to believe homosexuality is a genetic disposition, the Bible states it is the result of an unrestrained pursuit of vile passions and burning lusts. As our society continues to remove restraints against sexual sins, individuals will continue to plunge themselves into a cesspool of perverse and unnatural activities in an effort to pursue pleasure.

Of course, there are other sins caused by the lust of the flesh. These should be enough to show us how fleshly lusts war against our soul.

How to Overcome the Lust of the Flesh

Christians continue to be tempted to sin, so we must learn how to win this war waged against our soul. We are to be active in this conflict. The grace of God teaches us to deny worldly lusts through a practice of self-denial and self-control (Titus 2:11-12). The following are some suggestions of how we can overcome the lust of the flesh through the practice of self-denial and self-control.

1. **Have a "can do" attitude.** "I can do all things through Christ who strengthens me" (Phil. 4:13). The fact that God requires us to overcome lusts means we can. If we do not think we can do it, we defeat ourselves before we start. Whatever desire we struggle with, we must develop a determination to overcome it. We must see it as something we can accomplish.

2. **Pray.** If we know we have a problem with a temptation or sin, we can pray unto God for help in overcoming it. God wants to help us resist temptation. He knows how to deliver us out of temptation (2 Peter 2:9). He makes a way for us to escape our temptations (1 Cor. 10:13).

   The Lord encouraged His disciples to pray as a means of defeating temptation.

   "And do not lead us into temptation, but deliver us from the evil one…" (Matt. 6:13).

"Watch and pray, lest you enter into temptation. The spirit indeed is willing, but the flesh is weak" (Matt. 26:41).

3. **Walk in the spirit.** "I say then: Walk in the Spirit, and you shall not fulfill the lust of the flesh. For the flesh lusts against the Spirit, and the Spirit against the flesh; and these are contrary to one another, so that you do not do the things that you wish" (Gal. 5:16-17). The key to overcoming lust of the flesh is learning to "walk in the Spirit," to be willing to live according to the direction or the teaching of the Holy Spirit as revealed in the word of God. So long as one is making a purposeful effort to live according to the teachings of the Holy Spirit, he will not act upon his sinful desires.

We have a choice of two paths to walk (Rom. 8:1, 5-9). The two are incompatible. One excludes the other. The carnal mind (flesh) is not subject to the law of God, but the mind walking in the Spirit is subject to the law of God. We need to fill our minds with the word of God and be determined to obey the will of God, not the desires of our flesh.

4. **Control our thoughts.** "For those who live according to the flesh set their minds on the things of the flesh, but those who live according to the Spirit, the things of the Spirit" (Rom. 8:5). Our minds are not our playground. We are to set our mind upon the things of the Spirit, not fulfilling the sinful desires of our mind (Eph. 2:3). Every thought must be brought into captivity to obedience to Christ (2 Cor. 10:5). We must set our minds on the things above, not on the sinful things of this world (Col. 3:1-2). We cannot dwell upon the things we cannot have. We cannot go "window shopping" for sin without giving in to our lust or making ourselves miserable.

5. **Arm ourselves with scripture.** The Lord has equipped us with the weapon we need to defeat these worldly lusts which war against our soul. When Jesus was tempted by the devil, He answered every temptation by saying "It is written." (Matt. 4:4, 7, 10). We can cleanse our ways and guard ourselves against sin by hiding God's word in our heart (Ps. 119:9-11). If God's word is in our heart, we will be prepared to use it as a means of resisting temptation.

6. **Consider ourselves dead to sin.** "I have been crucified with Christ; it is no longer I who live, but Christ lives in me; and the life which I now live in the flesh I live by faith in the Son of God, who loved me and gave Himself for me" (Gal. 2:20). Paul put to death his self-will the day he became a

We cannot go **"window shopping"** for sin without **giving in** to our lust or making ourselves **miserable**.

Christian. From that day forward, he sought to fulfill Christ's will in his physical body. Like Paul, all of those who belong to Christ have crucified the flesh with its passions (Gal. 5:24). Crucifixion is an execution. There is no peaceful way for these warring parties (the flesh and the Spirit) to co-exist. The "enemy within the gates" must be put to death.

When we were baptized, the old body of sin was buried (Rom. 6:1-6). Why would we go dig it up? Sin is not to reign in our mortal bodies (vv. 11-12). The old man of sin is dead and buried. The new man lives to serve Christ. We cannot go back to our old way of living.

> Christians who do not practice **self-control** act as if they have **no choice** but to indulge in the sins of the world.

7. **Consider ourselves a slave to God.** We were slaves to sin, but when we obeyed the gospel, we were set free from sin and became enslaved to the One who set us free (Rom. 6:16-17). Slaves have no choice but to serve their master. Christians who do not practice self-control act as if they have no choice but to indulge in the sins of the world. Those who understand they are now servants of Christ realize they have no choice but to abstain from worldly lusts.

8. **Do not put ourselves in harm's way.** Peter tells us to abstain from these fleshly lusts which war against our soul (1 Pet. 2:11). To abstain does not mean we get as close to them as we can. It means we are to get away from them and stay away from them.

    "But put on the Lord Jesus Christ, and make no provision for the flesh, to fulfill its lusts" (Rom. 13:14). We are not to give ourselves a chance of being tempted, of exciting the lust of the flesh. We must end the battle before it ever begins. If we have a problem with a sin, we must stay away from the people, places, and things tempting us to fulfill these strong desires. This is especially hard in our society, but it is essential.

    When we find ourselves in harm's way, we must take the way of escape and get out before we commit the sin (Gen. 39:11-12; 1 Cor. 6:18; 2 Tim. 2:22).

9. **Make ourselves accountable.** "Confess your trespasses to one another, and pray for one another, that you may be healed. The effective, fervent prayer of a righteous man avails much" (James 5:16-17). Knowing we will have to give an account to another person can serve as a strong deterrent against sin and could help motivate us to a better practice of self-control.

10. **Consider our example.** "You are the salt of the earth; but if the salt loses its flavor, how shall it be seasoned? It is then good for nothing but to be thrown out and trampled underfoot by men" (Matt. 5:13). A Christian's influence is a very powerful thing, but it can also be a very fragile thing. What would brethren, family, friends, neighbors, etc., think of us if they knew we did not practice self-denial and pursued the lusts of the flesh? Are the immediate, temporal consequences of our sins painful enough to motivate us to control ourselves?

11. **Learn to tell ourselves "no."** "If anyone desires to come after Me, let him deny himself, and take up his cross, and follow Me" (Matt. 16:24). The first step of following Jesus is learning to deny ourselves—to tell ourselves "no." Ultimately, we are the only person who can do this. No one, not even God, can keep us from fulfilling the lust of the flesh. While people can help us, the battle with lust is a personal battle we must fight ourselves. We have to be the ones to tell ourselves "No."

Conclusion

Fleshly lusts war against our soul. They entice the enemy within (the flesh). Thus, overcoming lust is both an internal battle and a life-long battle. However, it is a battle God expects us to win by practicing self-denial and self-control. We need to stop waving the white flag of surrender to sin and take the battle for our soul seriously.

References

Barclay, William. *Flesh And Spirit*. Grand Rapids, MI: Baker Book House, 1976. 21-22. Print.

Sachs, Carl. *World History of the Dance*. New York: W.W. Norton & Company, 1937. Print.

Thayer, Joseph H. *Thayer's Greek-English Lexicon of the New Testament*. Peabody, MA: Hendrickson Publishers, 1996. 79-80. Print.

Questions

1. Identify the three avenues of temptation (1 John 2:16). _____
    _____
    _____

2. What does the word "lust" mean and how is it used in the New Testament? _____
    _____
    _____

3. Why is overcoming the lust of the flesh difficult? _____
    _____
    _____

4. What makes fleshly lusts our enemy (1 Pet. 2:11)? _____
    _____
    _____

5. Describe how one is tempted to sin. What role does lust or desire play in temptation
    (James 1:14-15)? _____
    _____
    _____

6. Name some sins produced by lust. Provide Scriptures with your answers. _____
    _____
    _____

7. How does dancing lead to sexual sins? _____
    _____
    _____

8. What effect did the sight of a naked woman have upon David (2 Sam. 11:2-4)? _____
    _____
    _____

9. What kinds of clothing are immodest (attract and invite sexual attention)? _____
    _____
    _____

10. Name at least two ways mixed swimming excites the lust of the flesh? _____
    _____
    _____

11. How do we know God wants to help us overcome temptation (Matt. 6:13; 2 Pet. 2:9; 1 Cor.
    10:13)? _____
    _____

12. How do we "walk in the Spirit" (Gal. 5:16-17)? _____

_____

_____

13. Where are we to "set our minds" (Rom. 8:5; Col. 3:1-2)? _____

_____

_____

14. What did Jesus use to resist temptation (Matt. 4:4, 7, 10)?_____

_____

_____

15. How is a Christian to "crucify the flesh with its passions" (Gal. 5:24)? _____

_____

_____

16. What is a Christian to do when he finds he is being tempted to sin (1 Cor. 6:18, 10:13)?

_____

_____

What do we know about the flesh?

Read Romans 8:5-8 and answer the following true or false questions about the flesh.

1. _____ A spiritual man can set his mind on the things of the flesh (v. 5).

2. _____ The flesh is opposed to the Spirit (v. 5).

3. _____ The consequences of the flesh are death (v. 6).

4. _____ Following the flesh can lead to life and peace (v. 6).

5. _____ The flesh is an enemy of God and is hostile to the things of God (v. 7).

6. _____ If necessary, the flesh is capable of submitting to the will of God (v. 7).

7. _____ A fleshly minded person can please God (v. 8).

8. _____ It is possible to follow the flesh and still belong to Christ (v. 9).

PRIDE

The word "pride" has several meanings. One definition is "proper respect for oneself; sense of one's own dignity or worth; self-respect" (Guralnik). Another definition is "delight or satisfaction in one's own or another's achievements" *(Ibid)*. We often use the word "pride" in this positive sense today. We take "pride" in things like a job well done. We tell our children we are "proud" of them. Everyone needs a sense of self-respect and self-worth.

However, there is another definition of "pride" that is not so appealing: "an overhigh opinion of oneself; exaggerated self-esteem; conceit; arrogance" *(Ibid)*. Negative pride develops with an exaggerated view of one's own self worth.

It is interesting to note the Bible never uses the words "pride" and "proud" in a positive sense. Instead, the Bible warns us against pride and encourages us to overcome it.

Overcoming our pride—learning to master it instead of it mastering us—is essential if we want to please God and go to heaven. However, overcoming pride is difficult when we consider the nature of the world in which we live. We are constantly bombarded by concepts such as "self-esteem," "self-worth," "self-image," "self-motivation," "learning to love ourselves," etc. The world caters to our sense of pride, which makes overcoming pride an uphill battle.

In this lesson, we will consider some of the serious dangers of pride, and then we will consider ways we can overcome sinful pride.

Problems with Pride

1. **Pride brings destruction.** "Pride goes before destruction, and a haughty spirit before a fall" (Prov. 16:18). Pride leads us to act without considering the long-term consequences of our actions—only the immediate satisfaction of our selfish desires. One who is motivated by pride walks into a snare. "A man's pride will bring him low…" (Prov. 29:23).

2. **Pride is deceptive.** "Do you see a man wise in his own eyes? There is more hope for a fool than for him" (Prov. 26:12; cf.

Every sin we will consider in this series is based upon **pride**; thus, overcoming pride will help us to **overcome sin**.

Focused upon **ourselves**, we will not care about the **feelings of others**, nor will we consider the impact that our **harsh words and actions** have upon others.

Obad. 3). Pride focuses upon self. As such, it prevents us from seeing things clearly.

Pride deceives us about *ourselves*. It prevents us from seeing ourselves as we really are. It over-exaggerates our good qualities while blinding us to our faults (Rev. 3:17).

Pride deceives us about *others*. "Let nothing be done through selfish ambition or conceit, but in lowliness of mind let each esteem others better than himself. Let each of you look out not only for his own interests, but also for the interests of others" (Phil. 2:3-4). Because of pride, we will see others as less important than ourselves. We will not care about the feelings of others nor consider the impact our harsh words and actions have upon them. Pride will not allow us to admit we have wronged another and seek to repair broken relationships (Matt. 5:23-24).

Pride deceives us about *God*. "The wicked in his proud countenance does not seek God; God is in none of his thoughts" (Ps. 10:4). The proud man sees himself as strong, independent, and self-sufficient. He does not see his need for God, nor does he consider the fact he has sinned against God. As such, he is woefully unprepared to meet God in judgment.

Pride deceives us about the *direction of our life*. "There is a way that seems right to a man, but its end is the way of death" (Prov. 14:12). Men who refuse to acknowledge their need for God often feel confident in finding their own way through life. They bounce from one philosophy to another (Acts 17:21), calling evil good and good evil (Is. 5:20), and end up traveling down the well-worn path to destruction (Matt. 7:13).

3. **Pride is an avenue of temptation.** Because of its deceptive nature, pride is a perfect avenue through which Satan tempts us to sin (1 John 2:15-17). Temptation comes, not just through the lust of the flesh and the eyes, but also by stroking our ego and telling us we need to better ourselves. This is one of the ways Satan tempted Eve to eat the forbidden fruit. He appealed to her pride when he told her, "For God knows that in the day you eat of it your eyes will be opened, and you will be like God, knowing good and evil" (Gen. 3:5). When she saw the tree was "desirable to make one wise" (v. 6) she took of the fruit and ate, thus sinning against God.

One way or another, all sin has its roots in pride. All sin involves what "I" want to do, satisfying self—not what God wants me to do, or what others need.

4. **Pride is a sin.** "A haughty look, a proud heart, and the plowing of the wicked are sin" (Prov. 21:4). Pride is a sin because it removes man's need for God. As our Creator, God has some rights over us. Pride strips God of these rights. Pride stands in the way of man rendering the praise and obedience due unto God. Pride will eventually make man out to be his own god.

   God's attitude toward the pride of man should alert us to the seriousness of this sin. God hates the proud (Prov. 6:16-17). He resists the proud (James 4:6) and finds them to be an abomination (Prov. 16:5).

How to Overcome Pride

Pride can be overcome by humility. "God resists the proud, but gives grace to the humble" (James 4:6). Humility does not come naturally or easy, especially in our self-centered society. The following are suggestions on how we can develop humility and thus overcome pride.

1. **We must learn to see ourselves in comparison to God.** "For if anyone thinks himself to be something, when he is nothing, he deceives himself" (Gal. 6:3). When we compare ourselves to ourselves, or to others around us, we can get an over-exaggerated, unrealistic view of our importance. However, when we learn to compare ourselves to the glory, majesty, and holiness of God, we will take the first step towards developing humility.

   In the Bible, when men saw the glory of God, they were overwhelmed and confessed their own unworthiness (Is. 6:1-5). Abraham was a great man, but when he was in the presence of God, he referred to himself as "dust and ashes" (Gen. 18:27).

   Jesus began the Beatitudes with "Blessed are the poor in spirit, for theirs is the kingdom of heaven" (Matt. 5:3). That is—blessed is the man who realizes that, before God, he is spiritually bankrupt. Such a person has taken the first step in entering the kingdom of heaven.

2. **We must realize our dependence upon God.** We would be nothing without God (Acts 17:24-25, 28). We are dependent upon Him for our next meal and even our next breath (Ps. 104:27-30). Tomorrow's accomplishments are not by the might of man, but by the grace of God (James 4:13-15). Dependence helps us develop humility because there is no room for arrogant boasting when one is living in a state of dependence.

> When we learn to compare ourselves to the **glory, majesty, and holiness** of God, we will take the first step towards **developing humility**.

3. **We must pursue humility.** Humility is more than just a feeling. Some people believe just because they feel a certain way it means they are that way. This is not true. Things can humble us and make us feel small or insignificant, but this feeling is not humility.

   Humility is a state of mind. The apostle Paul spoke of "serving the Lord with all humility of mind" (Acts 20:19 KJV). Humility has to do with the way we think (Rom. 12:3), not the way we feel. Peter tells us to be "clothed with humility" (1 Pet. 5:5). This means humility is a state of mind we choose to "put on." He goes on to tell us, "Therefore humble yourselves under the mighty hand of God, that He may exalt you in due time" (v. 6). This is a command we must obey. Humility does not come naturally, nor will we obtain it accidentally. We must pursue humility. We must make it our life's aim and goal.

4. **We must allow life's trials to humble us.** The trials of life can teach us how to be humble, if we will learn from them (James 1:2-4). It all has to do with how we choose to respond to these trials. Trials can help us see our need for God, or they can drive us away from God. If we allow the struggles and difficulties of life to humble and perfect us, God will exalt us. "Humble yourselves in the sight of the Lord, and He will lift you up" (James 4:10).

5. **We must possess a servant's mind and live a servant's life.** Jesus is our example of achieving humility through servanthood. "Yet it shall not be so among you; but whoever desires to become great among you, let him be your servant. And whoever desires to be first among you, let him be your slave—just as the Son of Man did not come to be served, but to serve, and to give His life a ransom for many" (Matt. 20:26-28).

   We are to have the same mind that caused Jesus to empty Himself of His own will and serve the Father for the benefit of others (Phil. 2:5-8). Humility must be put into action. We must learn to see the needs of others, but we must also learn to give ourselves to meet those needs. Getting in the habit of serving others will help us to develop humility.

Conclusion

The Bible spares no detail in warning us of the danger and seriousness of sinful pride. God resists pride because pride resists God. Pride elevates man to the place of God while blinding him to the destruction he will have to suffer.

We must overcome sinful pride in order to be pleasing to God. The choice to overcome pride will determine our eternal destiny. "For whoever desires to save his life will lose it, but whoever loses his life for My sake and the gospel's will save it" (Mark 8:35). If we, in our pride, seek to save our temporal life from the restraints of God's Word, we will lose our soul. However, if we overcome pride in this physical life and abide by God's Word, we will enter into heaven when this life is over.

References

Guralnik, David B. *Webster's New World Dictionary of the American Language.* New York, NY: 1986.

Questions

1. Does the Bible ever use the word "pride" in a positive way?_____
    _____
    _____

2. How does pride bring destruction? _____
    _____
    _____

3. How does pride deceive us about ourselves? _____
    _____
    _____

4. How does pride deceive us about others?_____
    _____
    _____

5. How does pride deceive us about God? _____
    _____
    _____

6. How does Satan use our pride as a means to tempt us to sin (1 John 2:16; Gen. 3:5-6)?
    _____
    _____

7. Can you think of a sin NOT connected to pride? _____
    _____
    _____

8. How is pride a sin against God? _____
    _____
    _____

9. What is God's attitude toward prideful men (Prov. 6:16-17, 16:5; James 4:6)?_____
    _____
    _____

10. What virtue is the opposite of pride (James 4:6)? _____
    _____
    _____

11. How did Isaiah react to being in the presence of God (Is. 6:1-5)? _____
    _____
    _____

12. How does a state of dependence help us develop humility? _____

_____

_____

13. Why must we pursue humility (Rom. 12:3; 1 Pet. 5:5-6)? _____

_____

_____

14. How can life's trials humble us (James 1:2-4)? _____

_____

_____

15. How can serving others help us develop humility? _____

_____

_____

Match the Bible verse with its teaching on pride.

1. Prov. 11:2   _____ stirs up strife

2. Prov. 16:5   _____ his soul is not upright in him

3. Prov. 16:18   _____ has deceived you

4. Prov. 21:24   _____ God resists the proud

5. Prov. 26:12   _____ an abomination to the Lord

6. Prov. 28:25   _____ more hope for a fool

7. Jer. 13:15   _____ then comes shame

8. Obad. 3   _____ goes before destruction

9. Hab. 2:4   _____ "Scoffer" is his name

10. James 4:6   _____ do not be proud

ANGER

All of us get angry from time to time. It is a natural way for us to react to things that happen to us. The Bible speaks numerous times of the anger and wrath of God. Jesus is described as having and exercising what we recognize as anger (John 2:13-17). The Bible even tells us we can be angry (Eph. 4:26). How then can we identify anger as a characteristic that does not belong in the life of a Christian?

Understanding what anger is will help us understand why it is unfitting in the life of a Christian. There are two Greek words translated as "anger" in the New Testament. The first word, *orge*, originally referred to any natural impulse, desire, or disposition. Over time, it came to signify anger as being the strongest of all passions. The second word, *thumos*, indicates a more agitated condition, an outburst of wrath resulting from inward indignation. It is a strong emotion that quickly blazes up, and then quickly subsides. The difference between the two words is while *thumos* is more volatile in its manifestation, *orge* is deep-seated and long lasting in its nature. Neither one of these characteristics is fitting for a child of God.

Anger is like a fire. If controlled, fire can do us much good, but if it gets out of control, it can do much damage. Some people can control their anger, and thus can do much good with their words and influence. However, some Christians seem to have a hard time controlling their anger. This is not the way God wants His children to act. In this lesson we will consider some reasons why it is wrong to be given to anger, and then we will discuss some things we can do to overcome a problem with anger.

What is wrong with uncontrolled anger?

1. **Anger leads to sin.** "Be angry, and do not sin: do not let the sun go down on your wrath, nor give place to the devil" (Eph. 4:26-27). This passage is not so much a license for anger as it is a warning about the connection between anger and sin. Remember, anger is defined as one of the strongest of man's passions. We are not to let our anger get the best of us, blind us to our senses and reason, and lead us to sin. "An angry man stirs up strife, and a furious man abounds in transgression" (Prov. 29:22).

We can see why anger is a **dangerous** characteristic for us to possess when we realize it is such a **strong avenue** for temptation and sin.

Someone may reason, "Well, I don't **fly off the handle** and explode in violent outbursts. I may hold on to my feelings of anger and resentment for a long time, but **at least I hold them in**."

Another may reply, "Well, I don't **sit and stew** over things that anger me. I may get a little upset and give someone a piece of my mind, but **at least I get it off my chest**."

Both of these attitudes are wrong.

When God rejected Cain's offering, Cain became angry. "Then the Lord said to Cain, 'Why are you angry? And why has your countenance fallen? If you do well, will not your countenance be lifted up? And if you do not do well, sin is crouching at the door; and its desire is for you, but you must master it'" (Gen. 4:6-7; NASV). God warned Cain his anger was opening the door to sin. The same thing is true for us. We can see why anger is a dangerous characteristic for us to possess when we realize it is such a strong avenue for temptation and sin.

2. **Anger resides in the same place in the heart as murder.** Jesus said, "You have heard that it was said to those of old, 'You shall not murder, and whoever murders will be in danger of the judgment.' But I say to you that whoever is angry with his brother without a cause shall be in danger of the judgment. And whoever says to his brother, 'Raca!' shall be in danger of the council. But whoever says, 'You fool!' shall be in danger of hell fire" (Matt. 5:21-22).

First, notice Jesus says those who are angry at their brother without a cause shall be in danger of the judgment. There are some legitimate reasons to be angry at a person, but more importantly, there are severe consequences to being angry without a cause.

Second, notice Jesus says the one who is angry without a cause is in danger of the same judgment as the one who has committed murder. Do not miss this point. The reason the man who is angry without a cause receives the same punishment as the murderer is because both anger and murder come from the same place. It is no accident Cain's anger led him to murder his brother (Gen. 4:8). In the heart, the person who is angry at his brother without a cause looks no different than the person who plans to commit murder. Because of this fact, John could write, "Whoever hates his brother is a murderer, and you know that no murderer has eternal life abiding in him" (1 John 3:15).

3. **Anger is condemned as a work of the flesh.** In Galatians 5:19-21, the apostle Paul tells us the works of the flesh are obvious. He then identifies some of them as being "hatred, contentions" and "outbursts of wrath." He concludes by saying, "those who practice such things will not inherit the kingdom of God."

Some Christians may say, "I may be a hothead. I may have a short fuse. I may fly off the handle and give people a piece of my mind, but that is just the way that I am." This may be the way they choose to be, but it is an indication they are led by their fleshly passions more than by the Holy Spirit, and as such they will not inherit the kingdom of God. Uncontrolled anger is a sin that will keep us out of heaven.

4. **Anger is characteristic of a fool.** "Do not hasten in your spirit to be angry, for anger rests in the bosom of fools" (Eccl. 7:9). Any behavior found in the heart of a fool is not fitting for a Christian.

   "A fool's wrath is known at once, but a prudent man covers shame" (Prov. 12:16). When have we made the biggest fools out of ourselves? Has it not been when we have spoken or acted out of anger? A prudent or wise person realizes it is foolish and shameful to be controlled by one's anger.

5. **Its fruits are hard to overcome.** Anger produces a bitter fruit. "For as the churning of milk produces butter, and wringing the nose produces blood, so the forcing of wrath produces strife" (Prov. 30:33). The results of anger are often a heavy burden for both ourselves and those around us. "A stone is heavy and sand is weighty, but a fool's wrath is heavier than both of them" (Prov. 27:3).

   Unfortunately, those with uncontrolled anger never seem to learn from their mistakes. "A man of great wrath will suffer punishment; for if you rescue him, you will have to do it again" (Prov. 19:19). They continue to act out of anger, and thus continue to bring shame and hardships upon themselves and others.

6. **Anger does not accomplish the will of God.** "So then, my beloved brethren, let every man be swift to hear, slow to speak, slow to wrath; for the wrath of man does not produce the righteousness of God" (James 1:19-20). Nothing should be more important to a Christian than to promote the kingdom of God and His standard of righteousness in this sinful world (Matt. 6:33). The Bible says it is impossible for the wrath of man to produce the righteousness of God. No good thing for the cause of Christ comes when we give in to and are governed by our anger.

How to Overcome Anger

Although anger is a strong and dangerous passion, it is not beyond our control. The Bible tells us there are some things we can do to overcome the exercise of sinful anger.

1. **Patience.** We must learn to control our anger by exercising patience with people and situations that try us.

   • "A quick-tempered man acts foolishly…" (Prov. 14:17).

No good thing for the **cause of Christ** comes when we give in to and are **governed** by our **anger**.

- "He who is slow to wrath has great understanding, but he who is impulsive exalts folly" (Prov. 14:29).

- "A wrathful man stirs up strife, but he who is slow to anger allays contention" (Prov. 15:18).

It is easy to become angry with others, even with our brethren. However, the apostle Paul tells us, "Therefore, as the elect of God, holy and beloved, put on tender mercies, kindness, humility, meekness, longsuffering; bearing with one another…" (Col. 3:12-13). The "elect of God" are not to be characterized by uncontrolled anger. Rather, we are to put on those things that will help us overcome anger: mercy, kindness, humility, meekness, patience, and a disposition to bear with or put up with our brethren.

2. **Forgiveness.** Paul continues the instruction "…and forgiving one another, if anyone has a complaint against another; even as Christ forgave you, so you also must do" (v. 13). Eventually, our brethren are going to do more than just make us angry. They are going to sin against us. When they do, we are to be quick to forgive them, just as we want Christ to be quick to forgive us. We need to learn to let things go. Nursing a grudge and stewing over past offenses will only lead to bitterness, resentment, and depression.

3. **Self-Control.** Aristotle is quoted as saying, "Anyone can become angry. But to become angry with the right person, to the right degree, at the right time, for the right purpose, and in the right way—this is not easy."

It takes great strength to control ourselves once the flames of anger have been stoked by an insult or wrong committed against us. "He who is slow to anger is better than the mighty, and he who rules his spirit than he who takes a city" (Prov. 16:32). We cannot control the things that happen to us, but we can always control how we will respond. The one who controls himself when provoked is stronger than the one who retaliates with anger and force.

"A fool vents all his feelings, but a wise man holds them back" (Prov. 29:11). When we allow anger to take control, our words will often bypass our brain unchecked and unrestrained. We need to pay extra attention to the way we act and speak when upset.

4. **A Soft Answer.** Part of controlling ourselves in times of anger is as simple as controlling the tone of our voice. "A soft answer turns away wrath, but a harsh word stirs up anger" (Prov. 15:1). It is hard to argue with someone who refuses to shout. When tempers are rising, Christians need to rise

The one who controls himself when **provoked** is stronger than the one who **retaliates** with anger and force.

above the temptation to fight and try to calm a volatile situation with their soft response.

5. **Discretion.** "The discretion of a man makes him slow to anger, and his glory is to overlook a transgression" (Prov. 19:11). Discretion is the ability to discern or to make a proper judgment before we react to a situation. It allows one to be careful about what he says and does. Such a characteristic can help one to be slow to anger.

The humorist Will Rogers once said, "People who fly into a rage always make a bad landing." We can only respond to a situation in a proper manner when we take the time to get all the facts and weigh them carefully. This will help us make sure we are not angry "without a cause" (Matt. 5:22). We can avoid anger by keeping our wits about us and thinking a matter through instead of responding purely out of emotion.

Conclusion

Fire has the potential of doing much good or much harm. It all depends upon our ability to keep it under control. The same thing is true of our anger. There are times when it is right to be angry, and exercising our anger in the right way can accomplish much good. However, left uncontrolled, anger can do unimaginable damage—some of which can never be repaired.

The potential for this damage should never be taken lightly by a Christian. If we have a problem with anger, we need to pray to God about it, and follow what His word says to do about it. Remember, those who fail to control their anger will not inherit the kingdom of God.

> We can only respond to a situation in a **proper manner** when we take the time to get **all the facts** and weigh them carefully.

Questions

1. In our lesson, we noted there are two basic Greek words for anger: *orge* and *thumos*. How do these words differ from one another?_____
    _____
    _____

2. How is anger like a fire?_____
    _____
    _____

3. What opened the door for Cain to commit the sin of murder (Gen. 4:5-7)? _____
    _____
    _____

4. Are there legitimate reasons to be angry at a person (Matt. 5:22)? _____
    _____
    _____

5. Why are murder and anger deserving of the same punishment? _____
    _____
    _____

6. Anger rests in the bosom of _____ (Eccl. 7:9).

7. What are some of the fruits of anger you have seen from your own experiences?_____
    _____
    _____

8. The wrath of man does not produce the _____ of God (James 1:20). Why not?
    _____
    _____

9. How does patience help us overcome anger?_____
    _____
    _____
    _____

10. What qualities and characteristics are we to show towards our brethren? (Col. 3:12-13)
    _____
    _____

11. What role does forgiveness play in overcoming sinful anger? _____
    _____
    _____

12. Who is mightier than one who conquers a city (Prov. 16:31)? _____

_____

_____

13. How can controlling the tone of our voice help to calm a volatile situation (Prov. 15:1)?

_____

_____

14. What is discretion and how does it help us to control our anger (Prov. 19:11)? _____

_____

_____

Thought Question

Identify some times Jesus showed self-control in the face of provocation.

WORRY

In Matthew 6:25-34, Jesus tells His disciples they are not to be characterized by worry and anxiety. Verse 25 says, "do not worry about your life" (NKJV). The New American Standard Version renders the phrase, "do not be anxious for your life," while the King James Version says, "take no thought for your life."

Nothing is wrong with thinking about the people and the things that are important in our life. Concern and preparation helps us avoid making mistakes, harming ourselves and our loved ones. Nothing is wrong with planning ahead. The sluggard is told to go to the ant and learn how to store up for the winter months (Prov. 6:6-8).

Jesus is not telling us it is wrong to think about our responsibilities, make plans for our future, or be concerned about our loved ones. Such would be reckless and irresponsible. Jesus is warning us against allowing these concerns to turn into anxiety and constant worrying.

The words "worry" and "anxious" are translated from the Greek word *merimnao*, which Strong defines as "to be anxious about." Thayer adds it is "to be troubled with cares," while Vine says it means "to have a distracting care." Webster's Dictionary defines the English word "worry" as "to feel distressed in the mind, be anxious, troubled, or uneasy."

Some Christians go beyond thought and care to distress and despair. They stew and fret over things out of their control, thus losing their appetite and sleep. They do it so much it becomes a part of who they are. They are characterized as "worry warts" or "fretful mothers." This is not the way God intends for His children to live. In Matthew 6:25-34, Jesus offers several good reasons for Christians not to be overcome with anxiety and distress. The Bible teaches there are things we can do to overcome the tendency to trouble ourselves with worries and cares.

What is wrong with worrying?

1. **Worrying is a sin** (Matt. 6:25, 31, 34). Three different times in this passage Jesus specifically commands us not to worry. When we worry, we disregard a direct command of the Lord, which is a sin. This command is as important and binding

When we give ourselves to **worrying**, we disregard a **direct command** of the Lord, which is a sin.

A **tendency to worry** is an indication we do not have the **basic elements** necessary to be **pleasing** to God.

as the prohibitions against lying, stealing, murder, adultery, blasphemy, etc.

2. **Worrying shows a lack of faith in God** (vv. 26, 28-30). Jesus says worry is the result of a lack of faith (v. 30). We must have faith in order to be pleasing unto God (Heb. 11:6). Worrying indicates we do not have the essential elements to be pleasing to God. We must trust Him to keep His promises. If our Heavenly Father feeds the birds and clothes the grass, can we not trust Him to look out for our well-being as His children (Matt. 7:9-11)? When we give ourselves to worry, we are telling God we do not think He can keep His promise and take care of us.

3. **Worrying accomplishes nothing** (v. 27). Worrying is like sitting in a rocking chair: it gives you something to do, but it does not take you anywhere. No one can add anything to his life by worrying about his life. Worry cannot add inches to our height or years to our life. In fact, just the opposite is true. Excessive worrying can impair our health and shorten our life.

4. **Worrying is what the Gentiles do** (vv. 31-32). When we worry, we are living more like a heathen than like a child of God. Those without the Lord have a reason to worry because they do not know or believe their Creator is watching out for them. They think they are on their own. We know we are not on our own. We have a Heavenly Father who watches out for us and takes care of us.

5. **Worrying distorts our priorities** (v. 33). Many things are important in our lives: the welfare of our family and loved ones, our health, the future of our country, etc. However, for the child of God, nothing should be more important than the kingdom of God. The time and energy we waste worrying about the things of life should be spent upon pursuing things related to the kingdom of God.

6. **Worry is a thief** (v. 34). Our English word "worry" is derived from an Old English word meaning "to strangle." Worrying does just that—it strangles the life out of us. Worry immobilizes us by unsettling our minds with real or imagined problems. It distracts us, robbing us of our time, mental energy, sleep, peace, and joy. However, this thief can only steal from us if we cooperate.

Worry robs us of our rightful service to the Lord. Martha's troubles and worries caused her to be distracted from what was really important (Luke 10:38-42). It robbed her of peace of mind and an opportunity to learn with her sister at the feet of Jesus. The Lord said the cares of the world choke the word out of man's heart, thus rendering it unfruitful (Matt. 13:22).

How to Overcome Worry

Christians who have a problem with worrying should not allow it to remain a part of their character. We cannot excuse sin in our life by saying, "This is just the way I am." We can and must change, but it will require some effort. What can we do to overcome the sin of worry?

1. **Increase our faith.** If worry is an indication of a lack of faith on our part, then we must increase our faith. This is done by spending time reading and meditating upon God's word (Rom. 10:17).

   Worry is also a lack of trust. What do we have to worry about if we believe God is both willing and able to care for us and provide for us? We need to develop a real trust in the God Who has proven His faithfulness, and take comfort in His promises (Rom. 8:32; 1 Cor. 10:13; Phil. 4:19).

2. **Prayer.** King Hezekiah did the right thing when a powerful enemy threatened his nation. He took the threatening letter Sennacherib had written and "spread it before the Lord" in prayer (2 Kings 19:14). The Lord granted Hezekiah and Jerusalem deliverance, not because of the king's military power, but because Hezekiah trusted in God to take care of the situation (v. 20).

   The apostle Paul promises the peace of God that surpasses all understanding will guard our hearts and minds, causing us to be at rest and free from worry—but only after we take our worries to God in prayer (Phil. 4:6-7). The apostle Peter encourages us to cast all cares upon God, "for He cares for you" (1 Pet. 5:7)

3. **Lean on a friend.** The Bible tells us of the value of friends, and perhaps there is no time when a friend is needed more than when we are struggling with troubles and cares. Some people choose to handle their problems alone, but the Bible teaches we are to seek the help of friends during times of sorrow and suffering (Prov. 17:17; Eccl. 4:9-11).

   The emotional weight of our problems is sometimes a burden we cannot bear alone. Our brethren are there to help us bear these burdens (Gal. 6:2). We can overcome worry by confiding in our brethren and asking for their prayers (James 5:16), knowing the "effective fervent prayer of a righteous man avails much."

Worry is **unfitting** for a child of God. It is **unnecessary**, **unproductive**, and **unworthy** of our time.

4. **Learn to live one day at a time.** God taught the children of Israel to live one day at a time when they collected the manna in the wilderness. Jesus taught us to have this same daily dependence upon God (Matt. 6:11, 34). Will Rogers once said, "Worrying is like paying on a debt that may never come due." Today is not an opportunity to recall yesterday's failures or to worry about tomorrow's problems. It is a day to rejoice and be glad (Ps. 118:24).

5. **Do the right thing.** Only those who have done evil and have told lies have to worry about what they have said and done. If we do what is right and do it to the best of our ability, we have no reason to worry (Acts 24:16).

   Worry is sometimes the result of a lack of preparation on our part. If we will live responsible lives and fulfill our obligations to the best of our ability, we will not have a reason to worry.

6. **Learn to be content.** Paul said he had learned to be content (Phil. 4:11-13). Some people worry about the things that can possibly happen to them: losing their job, losing their health, losing their loved ones, etc. We need to learn to enjoy what we have while we have it and learn to make the best of any situation in which we find ourselves. When things seem the worst, we need to remember the Lord can help us through it ("I can do all things through Christ who strengthens me"). We can always strive to improve our situation, but this is never accomplished by worry. Some things in life can be changed for the better, but some things are out of our control. As one has said, "What cannot be cured has got to be endured."

7. **Remember we cannot control other people.** Some people worry about other people— what they will do or what will happen to them. There are some areas in our life in which we are responsible for others. Parents are responsible for their children. Employers are responsible for the livelihood of their employees. Governing officials are responsible to their constituents. All of us are responsible for the example we leave before others.

   However, we also know we cannot control other people. We can only control ourselves (Rom. 12:18). We must learn to let people make their own decisions and, sometimes, suffer the consequences of those decisions. This can be especially difficult for parents, and thus many parents worry about their children. We love our children, but we should not give ourselves over to worrying about situations and people that are out of our control.

Conclusion

It seems few people are immune to the temptation to worry about things. Jesus tells us such worrying is unfitting for a child of God because it is what unbelievers do. As such, it is unnecessary, unproductive, and unworthy of our time.

Worst of all, the kind of worrying we have been discussing in this lesson is a sin. If you look within your heart and see you have a problem with worry, you need to get it out. It does not belong in the heart of a child of God. Work hard on overcoming it. The Lord will help you.

Questions

1. What is the difference between concern and excessive worrying? _____
   _____
   _____

2. Why is excessive worrying a sin? (Matt. 6:25, 31, 34) _____
   _____
   _____

3. How does worrying indicate a lack of faith in God? _____
   _____
   _____

4. Which is more important to God: birds and grass or His children?_____
   _____
   _____

5. Why would the Gentiles worry about obtaining their necessities? (Matt. 6:31-32) _____
   _____
   _____

6. What happened to the seed falling upon the thorny ground? (Matt. 13:22) _____
   _____
   _____

7. How can we increase our faith and trust in God? _____
   _____
   _____

8. When will the peace of God guard our hearts and lives? (Phil. 4:6-7)_____
   _____
   _____

9. What does it mean to cast all our care upon God? (1 Pet. 5:7) _____
   _____
   _____

10. What did Jonathan do for David? (1 Sam. 23:16) _____
    _____
    _____

11. How can learning to live one day at a time help us overcome worry and anxiety?_____
    _____
    _____

12. How can maintaining a clear conscience help us overcome worry and anxiety? _____

_____

_____

13. What had Paul learned to do? (Phil. 4:11) _____

_____

_____

Fill in the Blank

1. "But seek _____ the _____ _____ _____ and His _____, and all these things shall be added to you" (Matt. 6:33).

2. "He who did not _____ His own Son, but delivered Him up for us _____, how shall He not with Him also freely _____ us _____ things?" (Rom. 8:32).

3. "No temptation has overtaken you except such as is common to man; but God is _____, who will not allow you to be tempted _____ what you are able, but with the temptation will also _____ ____ _____ _____ _____, that you may be able to _____ it" (1 Cor. 10:13).

4. "And my God shall supply _____ your _____ according to His riches in glory by Christ Jesus" (Phil. 4:19).

5. "But without _____ it is impossible to please Him, for he who comes to God must _____ that He is, and that He is a rewarder of those who _____ seek Him" (Heb. 11:6).

6. "Casting _____ your _____ _____ _____, for He cares for _____" (1 Pet. 5:7).

7. "This being so, I myself always strive to have a _____ _____ _____ toward God and men" (Acts 24:16).

8. "If it is _____, as much as depends on _____, live peaceably with all men" (Rom. 12:18).

COVETOUSNESS

We live in a society driven by covetousness. Television programs showcase the lives of the rich and famous. They encourage us to measure ourselves by their standards.

Society tells us how much money we have determines our importance and worth as an individual. Those who give in to this kind of thinking spend their time and money in an endless effort to "keep up with the Joneses." Why? Covetousness.

Advertisers spend billions each year to get our attention and appeal to us to spend money we don't have on products we don't need. Because of the availability of credit, there is no need to deprive ourselves of a lifestyle we want. However, the bills eventually come due, and many people (including some Christians) find themselves under a mountain of debt. Why? Covetousness.

Why are gambling profits in the billions of dollars every year? Why do lottery jackpots reach well into the hundreds of millions of dollars? Why are casinos appearing all across the nation? Why are so many people addicted to gambling? What makes pyramid marketing and "get rich quick" schemes so attractive? Covetousness.

The illicit desire to have the things we see is called "covetousness." The Bible has a lot to say about this sin and the trouble it can cause, but it also tells us how we can overcome the sin of covetousness.

What is covetousness?

Several Greek words convey the idea of covetousness in the New Testament. In this lesson, we will focus upon one—*pleoneksia*. This word is a compound word. The first part of the word, *pleon*, means "more," and the second part, *echo*, means "to have." Thus, the word covetousness literally means "more to have." Covetousness is the wish to have more than one possesses, or as one has defined it, "a greedy desire to have more" (Thayer 516). It is an unquenchable thirst to get more and more of something we think we need in order to be satisfied. Included in this word is the idea of one who shamelessly overreaches into areas and places which are not his in order to satisfy his desires.

pleoneksia: covetousness; literally, "more to have"

What is wrong with covetousness?

Why is the desire to have more a sin? Why is it dangerous? The Bible pulls no punches in exposing the real nature of the sin of covetousness. Covetousness is a sin which the New Testament "again and again most unsparingly condemns" (Barclay 233).

1. **It keeps evil company.** Notice the sins listed with covetousness in the New Testament.

   • "Do you not know that the unrighteous will not inherit the kingdom of God? Do not be deceived. Neither fornicators, nor idolaters, nor adulterers, nor homosexuals, nor sodomites, nor thieves, nor covetous, nor drunkards, nor revilers, nor extortioners will inherit the kingdom of God" (1 Cor. 6:9-10).

   • "But fornication and all uncleanness or covetousness, let it not even be named among you, as is fitting for saints" (Eph. 5:3).

   • "For men shall be lovers of their own selves, covetous, boasters, proud, blasphemers, disobedient to parents, unthankful, unholy, without natural affection, trucebreakers, false accusers, incontinent, fierce, despisers of those that are good, traitors, heady, highminded, lovers of pleasures more than lovers of God" (2 Tim. 3:2-4, KJV).

2. **It defiles a man** (Mark 7:20-23). The sin of covetousness is not a harmless attitude to harbor in one's heart. It stains a man's heart and character from the inside out, thus defiling every aspect of his life, for one's life proceeds from his heart (Prov. 4:23).

3. **It is idolatry.** "Therefore put to death your members which are on the earth: fornication, uncleanness, passion, evil desire, and covetousness, which is idolatry" (Col. 3:5). Idolatry is not just the making of a graven image. Any primary focus in our life is an idol when it replaces God.

   A dime is very small in size and monetary value. Yet if it is held up close enough to the eye, nothing else can be seen. For a covetous man, his money has become his god. He seeks happiness in money, devotes himself to accumulating things, and trusts in his wealth. He gives it his affection, love, and respect. Nothing else in the world matters to him because his money is all that he can see.

4. **It provokes the wrath of God.** Covetousness is listed among the sins that will bring the wrath of God upon mankind (Col. 3:6). Any sin which provokes the wrath of God must be avoided.

Any **primary focus** in our life is an **idol** when it **replaces God**.

5. **It is the root of many other sins.** Covetousness is such an overwhelming desire for what belongs to another, we often violate the laws of right and justice to obtain our desire. The following are just some of the sins we can commit when we are driven by covetousness.

- **Theft** (Josh. 7:20-21). Achan coveted the spoil and stole it.

- **Lying** (2 Kings 5:20-27). Elisha's servant Gehazi lied to Naaman and to Elisha.

- **Betrayal** (Matt. 26:14-16; John 12:4-6). Judas sold out the Lord, in part, because he felt the Lord had deprived him of money.

- **Murder and extortion** (Ezek. 22:12). Covetousness causes one to do violence against his neighbor in order to have what he has.

- **Departing from the faith** (1 Tim. 6:9-10). The love of money and the desire to become rich open the door to many temptations, which lead men away from their faith.

- **Brings suffering upon loved ones** (Prov. 15:27). One cannot fill his house with the fruits of greed and covetousness without his household reaping the consequences.

How to Overcome Covetousness

We can overcome covetousness. Paul said the Christians in Corinth had overcome it (1 Cor. 6:9-11), which means we can overcome it as well.

Seeing as how covetousness is a never-ending desire for things, the key to overcoming this sin is learning how to be satisfied with what we have. We call this "contentment." "Let your conduct be without covetousness; be content with such things as you have…" (Heb. 13:5). However, contentment does not come naturally or easily to many people. Paul had to learn how to be content (Phil. 4:11), and so must we. What can we do to learn contentment and thus overcome the sin of covetousness?

1. **Learn to trust in God.** The Hebrew writer connects contentment with trusting in God: "…For He Himself has said, 'I will never leave you nor forsake you.' So we may boldly say: 'The Lord is my helper; I will not fear. What can man do to me?'" (Heb. 13:5-6). In learning to be content, Paul also learned he could do all things through Christ (Phil. 4:13).

   Ironically, our money carries the slogan "In God We Trust." Most people trust in the money more than in the God

contentment: learning how to be satisfied with what we have

professed by our currency. The more money they have, the better they feel. This dependence upon an abundance of wealth in order to feel secure is not pleasing to God. Faith is more than just belief. We must move beyond a simple belief in God to develop a trust in God to provide for our needs. He will see to it that we have what we need (Ps. 37:25).

2. **Learn that life is not about accumulating things.** The world says, "He who dies with the most toys wins." Jesus said, "Take heed and beware of covetousness, for one's life does not consist in the abundance of things he possesses" (Luke 12:15). The amount of things we have or the number of dollars in our checkbook do not determine the real value and worth of our life. Life is about being a person of real character (Prov. 22:1), enjoying family and friends, having fellowship with God (Acts 17:27), and securing an eternal resting place for our soul (Matt. 16:26). None of these things can be bought with money.

3. **Learn to set our minds on the things above.** "Set your mind on things above, not on things on the earth" (Col. 3:2). As long as our minds are focused on the things of the world, we are going to be tempted with covetousness. However, if our minds are focused upon the things of heaven, our desire will be for the things of heaven, not for the temporary things of this world (Matt. 6:19-21).

4. **Learn to be satisfied.** Solomon exposed the problems faced by those who have great wealth (Eccl. 5:10-12). We do not need abundance. Nothing is wrong with trying to improve ourselves, but when covetousness is the motivation behind it, we have created a monster that will never be satisfied. The improving of ourselves will know no end. We will always have to have more. We need to learn to be satisfied with the blessings God has seen fit to bestow upon us (Prov. 30:7-9).

5. **Learn to deny self** (Matt. 16:24). Covetousness is an expression of self-centeredness. Content means learning to tell self, "No!" The world tells us to help ourselves to the things we see. We know better, but the lust of the eyes is hard to overcome. We see things we want. We see neighbors enjoying things, and we want them too. These desires for things must be put to rest.

6. **Learn to love our neighbor.** One thing making covetousness such a vile sin is it causes us to disregard the rights and needs of others in our pursuit of things. Covetousness will eventually do harm to our neighbor, but love never will (Rom. 13:8-10). If we love our neighbor, we will respect what is his and learn to rejoice in his blessings

Nothing is wrong with trying to **improve ourselves**, but when covetousness is the **motivation** behind it, we have **created a monster** that will never be satisfied.

instead of envying them. Covetousness is the very opposite of generosity, charity, and love. Love moves us to consider others, do for others, and look out for the best interests of others, which moves us away from self-centeredness.

Conclusion

Covetousness is not a harmless habit or characteristic. Covetousness is "the sin of the man who has allowed full play to the desire to have what he should not have, who thinks that his desires and appetites and lusts are the most important thing in the world, who sees others as things to be exploited, who has no god except himself and his desires" (Barclay 235).

If we have a problem with covetousness, we begin overcoming it right now by praying to God for help. Then, we need to do what the Bible says we must do in order to learn to be content.

References

Barclay, William. *New Testament Words*. London, England: SCM Press Ltd., 1964. 233, 235. Print.

Thayer, Joseph H. *Thayer's Greek-English Lexicon of the New Testament*. Peabody, MA: Hendrickson Publishers, 1996. 516. Print.

Questions

1. What is the literal meaning of the Greek word for "covetousness" (*pleoneksi*)?_____
    _____
    _____

2. Name some of the sins listed alongside "covetousness" in the New Testament._____
    _____
    _____

3. What warning did Jesus give regarding the sins from within a man (Mark 7:20-23)? _____
    _____
    _____

4. Why does God consider covetousness to be idolatry (Col. 3:5)?_____
    _____
    _____

5. What is coming upon those who are covetous (Col. 3:6)? _____
    _____
    _____

6. How do we know covetousness can be overcome (1 Cor. 6:9-11)? _____
    _____
    _____

7. What virtue does the Bible offer as a cure for covetousness (Heb. 13:5-6)? _____
    _____
    _____

8. How can learning to trust in God help us to learn to be content? _____
    _____
    _____

9. What warning did Jesus give against covetousness in Luke 12:15? _____
    _____
    _____

10. What problems are experienced by those who are wealthy (Eccl. 5:10-12)?_____
    _____
    _____

11. What role does self-denial play in overcoming covetousness?_____
    _____
    _____

12. What role does love play in overcoming covetousness? _____
_____
_____

13. Identify the other sins caused by covetousness:

Joshua 7:20-21 _____

2 Kings 5:20-27 _____

Matthew 26:14-16 _____

Ezekiel 22:12 _____

1 Timothy 6:9-10 _____

Proverbs 15:27 _____

Fill in the Blank

1. "But _____ and all _____ or _____, let it not even be _____ among you, as is fitting for saints" (Eph. 5:3).

2. "Keep your heart with all _____, for out of it spring the issues of _____" (Prov. 4:23).

3. "For the _____ _____ _____ is a root of all kinds of _____, for which some have strayed from the faith in their _____, and pierced themselves through with _____ sorrows" (1 Tim. 6:10).

4. "Let your conduct be without _____; be _____ with such things as you have. For He Himself has said, 'I will never _____ you nor _____ you'" (Heb. 13:5).

5. "I have been young, and now am old; yet I have not seen the righteous _____, nor his descendants _____ bread" (Ps. 37:25).

6. "And He said to them, 'Take heed and _____ of _____, for one's life does not consist in the _____ of the things he _____'" (Luke 12:15).

7. "The _____ of a laboring man is sweet, whether he eats little or much; but the _____ of the rich will not permit him to _____" (Eccl. 5:12).

8. "Love does no _____ to a neighbor; therefore love is the _____ of the _____" (Rom. 13:10).

HYPOCRISY

"In the New Testament there is no sin more strongly condemned than hypocrisy, and in popular opinion there is no sin more universally detested" (Barclay 140).

This observation is very true. Few words conjure up feelings of disgust and disdain in the hearts of men like the word "hypocrite!"

In the New Testament, the words "hypocrite" and "hypocrisy" are translated for a family of words referring to an actor or one who is playing a part. "The word *hypocrite* is based on the Greek theatrical words meaning 'actor' or 'to play a part.' The essential identity of hypocrites, therefore, is that they pretend to be something they are not" (Ryken, Wilhoit, and et al). A hypocrite, then, is a person who is pretending to be someone they are not; one whose actions contradict their stated or internal beliefs.

Jesus often clashed with the scribes and Pharisees, and several times He brought attention to their hypocrisy and condemned them for this sin. On one occasion, the Pharisees sent their disciples to Jesus and asked Him about paying taxes unto Caesar. Luke says that they sent "spies who pretended to be righteous" (20:20). When they came to Jesus, they said, "'Teacher, we know that You are true, and teach the way of God in truth; nor do You care about anyone, for You do not regard the person of men. Tell us, therefore, what do You think? Is it lawful to pay taxes to Caesar, or not?' But Jesus perceived their wickedness, and said, 'Why do you test Me, you *hypocrites?*'" (Matt. 22:16-18, emphasis mine—HR). According to Jesus, a hypocrite is a person who is pretending to be someone they are not.

The Problem with Hypocrisy

Why does this sin receive such a strong condemnation from Christ, and why do we need to be concerned about removing it from our heart?

1. **Hypocrisy is a form of lying.** The whole purpose behind playing the hypocrite is to make others believe something about us that is not true; to deceive them with regard to our character or our motives. God hates lying (Prov. 6:16-19) and will punish all liars (Prov. 19:5).

> The word **hypocrite** is based on the Greek theatrical words meaning **actor** or **to play a part**.

"Often 'I love you' is **glibly** expressed; a **sugary, syrupy sentiment** that is not there when needed; **brotherly love** results in **sincere commitment** to others, seen and displayed in **actions** and not just **words**."

–*Ronny E. Hinds, unpublished notes on Romans 12:9*

Hypocrisy and lying go hand in hand. Paul says that those who depart from the faith will be "speaking lies in hypocrisy" (1 Tim. 4:2). How natural it is for one who is living a lie to speak a lie.

"The hypocrite with his mouth destroys his neighbor" (Prov. 11:9). This is exactly what Satan did to Eve (Gen. 3:1-5). He played the hypocrite, pretending to care about her wellbeing while his intent was to destroy her with sin.

2. **Hypocrisy taints true love.** "Now the purpose of the commandment is love from a pure heart, from a good conscience, and from sincere faith" (1 Tim. 1:5). Love must come from a heart that is pure, a conscience that is good, and a faith that is pure. Paul encourages us to "let love be without hypocrisy" (Rom. 12:9). Love is the greatest virtue that a Christian can possess, but hypocrisy is of such a nature it can destroy all the good done out of love.

Our love for others must be sincere and fervent (1 Pet. 1:22, 4:8). Our motives must be transparent in our relationship with others. Love is known by the actions that it prompts. We are not to show love in word only, but also with kind and helpful deeds (1 John 3:18).

Hypocritical Love: The Example of Judas

When Jesus was in Bethany, Mary broke a flask of costly oil and began to anoint the body of Jesus. Judas Iscariot protested the wasteful action: "Why was this fragrant oil not sold for three hundred denarii and given to the poor?" (John 12:5). While the criticism made Judas look like a man who cared for the poor, the reality was "he was a thief, and had the money box; and he used to take what was put in it" (v 6). Judas hid his true motives by pretending to care about the poor.

It was dark when Judas went out with the mob to arrest Jesus. He gave the mob a sign so they would know whom to arrest: "Whomever I kiss, He is the One; seize Him" (Matt. 26:28). When Judas approached Jesus, he acted like he was a friend, but Jesus exposed his hypocrisy when He said, "Judas, are you betraying the Son of Man with a kiss?" (Luke 22:48).

3. **Hypocrisy does great harm to the cause of Christ.** Sometimes people criticize the Lord's church by saying it is "full of hypocrites." Often this criticism is an excuse one uses to avoid their responsibility towards God. However, the reality is sometimes Christians do play the hypocrite before

unbelievers, and such actions have a negative effect upon efforts to spread the gospel to those who are lost.

The failure of God's people to "practice what we preach" will cause the name of God to be blasphemed among unbelievers (Rom. 2:21-24). When we try to live with one foot in the Kingdom of God and the other foot in the sinful world, unbelievers will see God is not first in our lives. Our faith is not real to them, and the teachings of our Lord are not worthy to be followed; thus they have no interest in hearing and obeying the gospel.

While it is true God judges everyone individually for their own unfaithfulness, it is equally true the Lord warned against those who would be a stumbling block or an offense to others (Matt. 18:6-7). The hypocrite is a stumbling block to those who need to see the pure light of the gospel shining in a world of sin and darkness. How terrible it would be to discover our actions kept someone from becoming interested in obeying the gospel.

4. **Hypocrisy is contagious.** Not only does the hypocritical Christian have a negative influence upon unbelievers, he also has a negative influence upon his brethren. Like many other sins, hypocrisy is contagious.

   Paul says Peter acted like a hypocrite while he was in Antioch (Gal. 2:11-13). There is no doubt Peter's hypocrisy had a negative impact upon the Gentile Christians he began to shun, but his actions also influenced other Jewish Christians to play the hypocrite with him. Even Barnabas, the Son of Encouragement, imitated Peter's hypocrisy.

   In the Bible, "leaven" often refers to the spreading influence of sin (1 Cor. 5:6-7). Jesus said the "leaven" of the Pharisees was their "hypocrisy" (Luke 12:1). The Pharisees may have taught the Scriptures, but what they displayed in their daily lives was hypocrisy. The disciples needed to take heed they did not become like the Pharisees.

5. **The hypocrite will be destroyed.** Hypocrisy is a sin, and like all other sins, hypocrisy will result in punishment and the hypocrite will end up in Hell. In one parable, Jesus taught that an evil servant would be cut in two and appointed a portion with the "hypocrites" where there will be "weeping and gnashing of teeth" (Matt. 24:51). Hypocrisy is a form of lying, and all liars "shall have their part in the lake which burns with fire and brimstone" (Rev. 21:8).

   In the early church, two members named Ananias and Sapphira sold a possession, kept back part of the money for

> The hypocrite is a **stumbling block** to those who need to see the **pure light** of the gospel shining in a world of sin and darkness.

themselves, and brought the rest and laid it at the apostles' feet (Acts 5:1-11). God struck them dead. It was not wrong for them to keep back money for themselves. The problem is they wanted credit for giving everything to the Lord. Pretending to be more generous than they really were, Ananias and Sapphira sinned. They were hypocrites.

How to Overcome the Sin of Hypocrisy

Just as with other sins, one can overcome the sin of hypocrisy. There are different reasons that Christians pretend to be someone that they are not, so there are different things that can help one overcome this sin.

1. **Repent of our sin.** One reason Christians are hypocrites (act like people they are not) is because they are trying to hide sin in their life. They act righteously in an effort to make sure no one discovers their sinful secrets. Judas acted piously in an attempt to cover up the fact he was covetous and a thief (John 12:4-6). The Pharisees put much effort in acting righteously, but their hearts were actually full of sin (Matt. 23:25-26). Jesus taught the cleansing of the heart would lead to a righteous life.

   The proper way to deal with our sin is to repent (Acts 8:22), not to hide it under a veil of righteousness. Sin causes us embarrassment and leads us to feel the need to conceal it (Rom. 13:14; 1 Thess. 5:22; James 4:7-8). We must learn to overcome the temptation to commit sin.

2. **Stop seeking the praise of men.** Some Christians are hypocrites because they try to please both God and man. We cannot divide our loyalty between two masters (Matt. 6:24). We are to seek God with our whole heart (Psa. 119:10), not with divided affections. The hypocrite seeks to do this: acting one way on Sunday to please his God and his brethren, then acting a different way the rest of the week in an effort to enjoy the pleasures of the world and to receive praise from worldly minded people. This balancing act may fool men, but it will not fool God. Friendship with the world is enmity with God (James 4:4).

   We must choose godly character over worldly reputation. A mature Christian knows his duty is to please God—not man (Gal. 1:10). A hypocrite has sold out his integrity for the praise of men. A man of character will remain true to his convictions regardless of the cost.

   The Pharisees set themselves up as the most righteous and devout of the Jews. In their effort to keep their reputation, they fell victim to the temptation to keep up appearances at

> A hypocrite has **sold out** his integrity for the **praise of men**. A man of **character** will remain true to his **convictions** regardless of the **cost**.

all costs. Soon, the inward practice of their religion gave way to keeping up outward appearances. The Pharisees made an ostentatious practice of their religion for one purpose—for the praise of men. In doing so, the practice of their religion brought them no praise or reward from God (Matt. 6:1-6, 16-18, 23:5-7). Others will certainly see the good works we do in the practice of our religion (Matt. 5:16), but the result must be God is glorified, not ourselves. What is the motivation behind the things we do in our service to God and others?

3. **Practice what we preach.** Jesus exposed the hypocrisy of the scribes and Pharisees regarding their actions not matching their teaching. "Therefore whatever they tell you to observe, that observe and do, but do not do according to their works; for they say, and do not do" (Matt. 23:3). Notice Jesus did not disregard their teaching. Truth is truth—even out of the mouth of a hypocrite. We are to believe and obey the truth regardless of the character of the one who may happen to teach it. However, possessing the truth will do us no good personally if we fail to obey it.

Perhaps no man was in a better position to understand the truth regarding the acceptance of the Gentiles than the apostle Peter. He received visions from the Lord and witnessed the outpouring of the Holy Spirit as confirmation that God accepted the Gentiles (Acts 10). Peter even preached the truth on this subject (Acts 11:4-18, 15:7-11). However, he acted contrary to this understanding when he was in Antioch (Gal. 2:11-13). He did not practice what he preached, and Paul said he played the hypocrite.

Remember, the Jews possessed the law of God, but they dishonored God by failing to keep the law (Rom. 2:21-24). They were just as guilty of sin before God as were the Gentiles. The best way to overcome hypocrisy is to make sure our words and actions are always in harmony with the truth of God's word.

4. **Judge with righteous judgment.** It is hypocritical for a man to hold others to a higher standard than what he uses for himself. This was the point of Jesus' teaching in Matthew 7:1-5. "Judge not" is not a condemnation against a Christian ever making a judgment with regards to another person. The passage is a warning against hypocritical judgments. Jesus referred to the man with the plank in his eye as a "hypocrite." Why? This man, with an obvious fault (a plank, log, beam sticking out of his eye), felt the need to help another man remove a speck from his eye. He ignored or dismissed his glaring fault and pointed out a minute fault in another. According to the Lord, that makes one a hypocrite.

> We do not need to **overlook** sins, but we do need to be as **merciful** upon others as we would want them to be upon us.

Jesus spoke a similar truth when He rebuked the scribes and Pharisees for straining out a gnat and swallowing a camel (Matt. 23:24).

A hypocrite, in this sense, is one who condemns sin in others while ignoring sin that exists in their own life. They judge others by a harsh standard. They judge themselves and their loved ones by a lesser standard. We need to learn to judge righteous judgment (John 7:24), and we need to apply it consistently and without prejudice or partiality (1 Tim. 5:21). We do not need to overlook sins, but we need to be as merciful upon others as we would want them to be upon us (James 2:13). Everyone sins and falls short of the glory of God (Rom. 3:23). Eventually, unmerciful judgment makes everyone a hypocrite.

5. **Get into the habit of telling and living the truth.** Hypocrisy is a form of lying. If we have a problem with hypocrisy, we need to stop lying through both our words and our actions. Like Paul, we are to live openly and honestly with all men (2 Cor. 8:21). We need to learn to be content with our state of life (Phil. 4:11), rather than feeling the need to impress others and live up to cultural expectations. We need to stop giving in to the temptation to have others believe we are something we are not.

Conclusion

Acting like someone we are not was fun to do as a child: to dress up in a costume and pretend like we were a historical figure or a super hero. Acting out a role in a play is innocent fun, and for those who are especially talented, acting can be an honorable profession. However, there is nothing honorable about someone playing the hypocrite.

Hypocrisy is a sin that received the Lord's strongest condemnation. It is a purposeful effort to deceive others with regards to our true character and motives. As with other sins, hypocrisy must be laid aside (1 Peter 2:1-3). Christians are to be the "real deal." We are to have a genuine faith (2 Tim. 1:5) and sincere love (2 Cor. 6:6; 1 Pet. 1:22). If we find we have a problem with this sin, we need to pray to God for forgiveness and take necessary steps to make sure we are not appointed a portion with the hypocrites (Matt. 24:51).

References

Barclay, William. *New Testament Words*. London, England: SCM Press Ltd., 1964. 140. Print.

Ryken, Leland, James C. Wilhoit, et al. *Dictionary of Biblical Imagery*. Downers Grove, IL: 1998.

Questions

1. In your own words, describe what a hypocrite is. _____
_____
_____

2. How is hypocrisy a form of lying? _____
_____
_____

3. How did Satan play the hypocrite with Eve (Gen. 3:1-5)? _____
_____
_____

4. From where must love come (1 Tim. 1:5)? _____
_____
_____

5. How did Judas show hypocritical love (John 12:5-6; Matt. 26:28)? _____
_____
_____

6. How do unbelievers react when believers are hypocrites (Rom. 2:21-24)?_____
_____
_____

7. Who encouraged Barnabas to play the hypocrite (Gal. 2:11-13)? _____

8. What was the leaven of the Pharisees (Luke 12:1)?_____
_____
_____

9. What will happen to hypocrites (Matt. 24:51; Rev. 21:8)? _____
_____
_____

10. How did Ananias and Sapphira play the hypocrite (Acts 5:1-11)? _____
_____
_____

11. Why is it foolish to try to cover up our sin (Num. 32:23)?_____
_____
_____

12. Who should a Christian strive to please (Gal. 1:10)? _____
_____

13. Who did Jesus call a "hypocrite" in Matthew 7:3-5? _____
   _____
   _____

14. How can contentment help us avoid hypocrisy (Phil. 4:11)? _____
   _____
   _____

The Characteristics of Hypocrisy Manifested by the Pharisees

Jesus reserved His harshest condemnation for the scribes and the Pharisees, who He repeatedly called "hypocrites." Describe the specific ways the scribes and Pharisees were acting as hypocrites in the passages below.

1. Matthew 6:1-6, 16-18, 23:5-7 _____
   _____

2. Matthew 23:3 _____
   _____

3. Matthew 23:14 _____
   _____

4. Matthew 23:16-22 _____
   _____

5. Matthew 23:23 _____
   _____

6. Mark 7:6-13 _____
   _____

7. Luke 12:54-56 _____
   _____

GOSSIP

God created man as a social being. For the most part, people do not like to be alone. As a rule, we like to be with other people and we like to talk to other people. The ability to communicate brings some great blessings to mankind, but the devil also uses human communication as a means of spreading sin and grief. We are all painfully aware of the damage that can be caused by our words.

The Bible addresses the dangers posed by the tongue. James says man's tongue is a fire and an unruly evil full of deadly poison (James 3:6, 8). Of all the sins committed with the tongue, there is one that is especially a problem for some Christians—the sin of gossip.

Webster's Dictionary defines "gossip" as "a person who chatters or repeats idle talk and rumors, especially about the private affairs of others" (Guralnik). Thus, gossip is idle talk and rumors about the private affairs of others. Closely related to gossip is the word "slander" which means "the utterance in the presence of another person of a false statement or statements, damaging to a third person's character or reputation" (Guralnik). The Bible also uses the words "talebearer" and "whisperer."

Like any other sin that brings one satisfaction and pleasure, gossip can be addictive to some people. Paul warned Timothy and Titus of the danger of some women becoming gossips and busybodies (1 Tim. 5:13; Titus 2:3). While these passages specifically mention women, we all know men can be equally guilty of this sin.

A problem with the sin of gossip is not to be accepted, excused, or overlooked. Like all other sins, one who has a problem with gossip must work hard to overcome this sin.

gossip:
a person who chatters or repeats idle talk and rumors, especially about the private affairs of others

The Damage Caused by Gossip

Gossip is not a harmless habit. The Bible warns of the damage that can be caused by gossip, slander, whispering, and talebearing.

1. **It reveals secrets.** "He who goes about as a talebearer reveals secrets, but he who is trustworthy conceals a matter" (Prov. 11:13, NASV). Notice some things about this verse. First, a talebearer is one who "goes about" looking to dispense his

> The **purpose** of these stories is not to **inform** and **forewarn** men, but to kindle strife for the **amusement** of the talebearer.

tales. There is nothing accidental about gossip or slander. It is a purposeful effort to harm another person. Second, this passage portrays the talebearer as one who has violated a trust. He has been trusted with a secret, the contents of which can damage an individual, and has chosen to violate this trust in order to enjoy the pleasure of spreading gossip. Such a violation can damage a friendship beyond repair (Prov. 18:19). A good man will honor a friend's confidence and protect a friend's reputation.

2. **It kindles strife.** "Where there is no wood, the fire goes out; and where there is no talebearer, strife ceases. As charcoal is to burning coals, and wood to fire, so is a contentious man to kindle strife" (Prov. 26:20-21). A talebearer is one who tells stories that ought not to be told. The purpose of these stories is not to inform and forewarn men, but to kindle strife for the amusement of the talebearer. God pronounced His hatred upon those who purposely sow strife among their brethren (Prov. 6:16-19). Christians are to be peacemakers, not troublemakers (Matt. 5:9; Heb. 12:14).

3. **It separates friends.** "An ungodly man digs up evil, and it is on his lips like a burning fire. A perverse man sows strife, and a whisperer separates the best of friends" (Prov. 16:27-28). Gossip, talebearing, and whispering are the tools used by one who is intent upon causing trouble. He digs up dirt on people, whispers it to a few individuals, and then watches the destruction spread like fire. False tales and revealed secrets can turn people against one another. The damage caused by gossip is so harsh it can even destroy the closest of friendships.

4. **It brings anger.** "The north wind brings forth rain, and a backbiting tongue an angry countenance" (Prov. 25:23). A backbiter is one who does not have the courage to challenge a person to their face. Instead of meeting them face to face in honest discussion or debate, they will spread lies and rumors behind their back. When these efforts are discovered, the injured party will often respond in anger. Uncontrolled anger and outbursts of wrath stir up strife and transgression (Prov. 29:22).

The King James Version renders Proverbs 25:23 as "The north wind driveth away rain: so doth an angry countenance a backbiting tongue." This is the opposite of the rendering in newer translations. While the meaning is opposite, it still states a truth. A talebearer is looking to peddle his wares. Meeting a slanderer and backbiter with indignation rather than acceptance will often "drive" them away. Indeed, "where there is no wood, the fire goes out…" (Prov. 26:20).

Gossips and backbiters would not be in business if people were not so willing to consume their product.

4. **It shows one to be a fool.** The involvement in any sin committed with our words indicates to others we are a fool. "He who restrains his words has knowledge, and he who has a cool spirit is a man of understanding. Even a fool, when he keeps silent, is considered wise; when he closes his lips, he is counted prudent" (Prov. 17:27-28, NASV). While a whisperer may try to hide his identity, he will eventually be exposed for what he is—a fool!

How to Overcome the Sin of Gossip

Gossip is not a harmless habit. Gossip is a sin that causes untold amounts of damage. A desire to engage in gossip should not be excused by saying "this is just the way I am," or rationalized by claiming that we are doing people a favor by informing them and warning them about others. Like all other sins, the Christian must strive to overcome the temptation to engage in gossip.

Gossip can be overcome through the practice of self-control: keeping our mouth closed, removing ourselves from the "grapevine," and learning to find joy in something other than being a talebearer. We would do good to ask the following questions before we repeat something.

1. **Is it true?** If it is not true, it is a lie. Slander, by definition, is telling something that is not true. A Christian is not to have anything to do with spreading a lie.

   "He who answers a matter before he hears it, it is folly and shame to him... The first one to plead his cause seems right, until his neighbor comes and examines him" (Prov. 18:13, 17). It is easy to draw an inaccurate conclusion when we only hear one side of the story. We would save ourselves some embarrassment and others some grief, if we would take the time to get all the facts before we act upon or repeat a matter.

2. **Is it going to build up or tear down?** "Therefore let us pursue the things which make for peace and the things by which one may edify another" (Rom. 14:19). Gossip and slander bring anger, contention, and strife. The tools of a talebearer will never contribute to peace and edification among brethren. Our words have great power for both good or evil. We are to pursue the things that build up our brethren, not tear them down.

   Sometimes negative things need to be said about others; people need to be warned, and important lessons can be

When one **sins against** us, we usually want to talk to everyone, **except** the one the **Lord** tells us.

learned from negative examples. However, great care and wisdom need to be exercised when talking to someone about the misdeeds of another person.

3. **Have I talked to them first?** "Moreover if your brother sins against you, go and tell him his fault between you and him alone. If he hears you, you have gained your brother" (Matt. 18:15). Private matters need to remain private. When one sins against us, we usually want to talk to everyone, except the one the Lord tells us. This is how gossip gets started. We can avoid gossip if we will follow the Lord's instructions.

Sometimes malicious gossip can be stopped if we will take the reports to the person who is the subject of the gossip. The talebearer rarely wants someone to investigate the facts regarding his story. He simply wants it to be believed and spread to others. If we care enough to spread a story, should we not care enough to get the facts straight first? If talebearers know we will "call them" on their facts, they will stop coming to us with gossip.

4. **Have I examined myself?** Jesus shows us the wisdom of examining ourselves before we get involved in the affairs of others (Matt. 7:3-5). Only a hypocrite will spread stories about the faults of others while displaying greater faults in his own life. We need to clean our own house before we try to clean someone else's house.

5. **Why am I *really* wanting to do this?** What is motivating me to tell this to someone else? Am I trying to achieve good, or am I getting some pleasure out of repeating this matter? The truth is some people engage in gossip simply because they enjoy it. "The words of a talebearer are like tasty trifles, and they go down into the inmost body" (Prov. 18:8, c.f. 26:22).

Some people act as if they have no choice but to repeat a matter. This simply is not true. "He who covers a transgression seeks love, but he who repeats a matter separates friends" (Prov. 17:9). We are not to ignore sin, but if we love the person and want what is best for them, we will conceal the matter from public view and spare our loved one much embarrassment. If we love the pleasure of gossip, we will repeat the matter and watch the destruction that follows.

6. **Is this what I would want done to me?** "Therefore, whatever you want men to do to you, do also to them, for this is the Law and the Prophets" (Matt. 7:12). We would not want people spreading lies and rumors about us, nor would we want friends to betray our trust and advertise our secret struggles and transgressions before others. If we do not want others doing this to us, we must not do it to others. If we mistreat others in the way we talk about them, we can expect others to do the same thing to us.

Conclusion

Gossip is a sin which seeks to destroy another person for our own selfish pleasure. It has always been unfitting for a child of God. "You shall not go about as a talebearer among your people..." (Lev. 19:16). If we find we have a problem with the sin of gossip, we should not overlook it or seek to excuse it. We need to work hard, overcome it, and become a Christian whose words are both pleasing to God and a constant source of encourage to others.

References

Guralnik, David B. *Webster's New World Dictionary of the American Language*. New York, NY: 1986.

Questions

1. Define the word "gossip." _____
   _____

2. Define the word "slander." _____
   _____

3. What is God's attitude towards one who sows discord (Prov. 6:16-19)? _____
   _____

4. Name two things produced by anger (Prov. 29:22). _____
   _____
   _____

5. How can a fool convince others he is wise (Prov. 17:27-28)? _____
   _____
   _____

6. Who are we to talk to first when we have been sinned against (Matt. 18:15)? _____
   _____

7. What are we to do when we discover we have sinned against another person (Matt. 5:23-24)?
   _____

8. What do we need to do before we "help" another person get a speck out of their eye
   (Matt. 7:3-5)? _____
   _____

9. How do some people view the words of a talebearer (Prov. 26:22)? _____
   _____

10. What was David's prayer in Psalms 19:14? _____
    _____

Consequences of Gossip

Identify the results of gossip mentioned in the following verses.

1. Prov. 11:13_____
   _____

2. Prov. 15:28 _____
   _____

3. Prov. 16:28 _____
   _____

4.   Prov. 17:27-28 _____

_____

5.   Prov. 20:19 _____

_____

6.   Prov. 25:23 _____

_____

7.   Prov. 26:20 _____

_____

Discussion Questions

1.   What is a busybody (1 Tim. 5:13)? _____

_____

2.   How can gossip separate the best of friends (Prov. 16:28)? _____

_____

3.   How can "getting all the facts" help us avoid the sin of gossip? _____

_____

4.   Is it ever necessary to say negative things about others? If so, how should we go about saying such things? _____

_____

5.   What is the difference between ignoring sin and "covering a transgression" (Prov. 17:9)?

_____

_____

FEAR

Psychologists tell us we are born with two fears—the fear of falling and the fear of loud noises. However, many of us soon learn many more fears. There are hundreds of phobias recognized today. Some of them are reasonable and common, while others seem very strange, but they are all very real.

- **Claustrophobia:** fear of confined spaces

- **Altophobia:** fear of heights

- **Aviophobia:** fear of flying

- **Hydrophobia:** fear of water

- **Arachnophobia:** fear of spiders

- **Ophidiophobia:** fear of snakes

- **Glossophobia:** fear of public speaking

- **Brontophobia:** fear of thunder and lightning

- **Coulrophobia:** fear of clowns

- **Dendrophobia:** fear of trees

- **Pentheraphobia:** fear of mother-in-law

- **Phronemophobia:** fear of thinking

- **Ecclesiophobia:** fear of church

- **Homilophobia:** fear of sermons

- **Panophobia:** fear of everything

The Bible uses the word "fear" in two ways. First, the Bible speaks of fear in the sense of reverence and respect. "Let us hear the conclusion of the whole matter: fear God and keep His commandments, for this is man's all" (Eccl. 12:13). This fear is good and wholesome, leading to knowledge (Prov. 1:7) and the salvation of our souls (Acts 10:35). The Bible also uses the word "fear" to speak of "a feeling of anxiety and agitation caused by the presence or nearness of danger, evil, pain, etc.; timidity; dread; terror; fright; apprehension" (Guralnik). This second understanding of fear will be the focus of this lesson.

Fear, in the sense of **reverence and respect** for God, is **good** and wholesome, leading to **knowledge** and the **salvation** of our souls.

This fear is not to be confused with caution. Fear of getting run over by a car causes us to be careful when crossing the street. Fear of getting burned causes us to be careful around a fire. This type of fear is normal and helpful. When fear paralyzes and renders us unproductive, it is not normal.

There are many different kinds of fears that trouble Christians. Fear of failure keeps us from trying new things (teaching Bible class, evangelism). Fear of the unknown keeps us from taking chances. Fear of insecurity calls God's love and care into question. Fear of criticism keeps us from doing anything, because everything we do can be criticized. God has not given us a spirit of fear (2 Tim. 1:7), but some Christians live in it. Why is it wrong for a Christian to be characterized by fear, and what can we do to overcome it?

What is wrong with fear?

"The fear of man brings a snare, but whoever trusts in the Lord shall be safe" (Prov. 29:25). Fear is not a harmless trait. It is the gateway to many troubles for man. Consider some of the snares caused by fear.

1. **It keeps one from confessing Christ.** We must be willing to confess Jesus is the Son of God (Matt. 10:32-33; Rom. 10:9-10). Fear of men can keep us from making this good confession. "Nevertheless even among the rulers many believed in Him, but because of the Pharisees they did not confess Him, lest they should be put out of the synagogue; for they loved the praise of men more than the praise of God" (John 12:42-43; cf. 7:13, 9:22). If we cannot muster the courage to confess our faith in Christ before men, we cannot be saved.

2. **It keeps our faith a secret.** Concerning Joseph, we read, "After this, Joseph of Arimathea, being a disciple of Jesus, but secretly, for fear of the Jews…" (John 19:38). How many secret disciples does the Lord have today? How many will go to judgment unprepared, never hearing the gospel because disciples were afraid and kept their faith a secret? We are to let our light shine, not hide it under a basket in fear (Matt. 5:14-16).

3. **It keeps one from obeying God.** King Saul had received a clear command from God. He was to "go and attack Amalek, and utterly destroy all that they have, and do not spare them. But kill both man and woman, infant and nursing child, ox and sheep, camel and donkey" (1 Sam. 15:3). Saul spared the king and the best of the livestock. When confronted by Samuel regarding his disobedience, Saul

How many sinners will go to judgment **unprepared**, having never heard the gospel because disciples were **afraid** and kept their faith a **secret**?

disgracefully said, "I have sinned, for I have transgressed the commandment of the Lord and your words, because I feared the people and obeyed their voice" (v 24).

Fear paralyzes us when faced with obstacles or undesirable responsibilities. The unprofitable servant buried his talent because he was afraid (Matt. 25:25) and suffered his master's wrath. The Lord's vengeance comes on "those who do not know God, and on those who *do not obey the gospel* of our Lord Jesus Christ" (2 Thess. 1:8; emphasis mine—HR).

4. **It makes one's life miserable.** Saul lost his kingdom as a result of his disobedience. When Samuel anointed David as the next king, "the Spirit of the Lord departed from Saul, and a distressing spirit from the Lord troubled him" (1 Sam. 16:14). Saul was never the same afterwards. He spent the rest of his life paranoid and obsessed with destroying David.

   "For God has not given us a spirit of fear, but of power and of love and of a sound mind" (2 Tim. 1:7). However, when one allows fear to rest in their heart, it soon erodes their "sound mind." Fear involves terror and dread (1 John 4:18). Afflicted by phobias, some make their lives miserable. This is no way for a Christian to live. We are more than conquerors in Christ (Rom. 8:37).

5. **It renders one useless in his service to God.** "And the Lord said to Gideon, 'The people who are with you are too many for Me to give the Midianites into their hands, lest Israel claim glory for itself against Me, saying, "My own hand has saved me." Now therefore, proclaim in the hearing of the people, saying, "Whoever is fearful and afraid, let him turn and depart at once from Mount Gilead."' And twenty-two thousand of the people returned, and ten thousand remained" (Judges 7:2-3). God could have chosen any means of reducing the number of men in Gideon's army. Why did He choose fear? Those who are fearful will have a negative influence upon the success of any people (Deut. 20:8). If overcome with fear, we are of no use to the Lord.

6. **It causes one to lose his soul.** Notice that cowardice tops the list of those who will suffer the second death in the lake of fire and brimstone: "But the cowardly, unbelieving, abominable, murderers, sexually immoral, sorcerers, idolaters, and all liars shall have their part in the lake which burns with fire and brimstone, which is the second death" (Rev. 21:8). Consider the sins associated with fear in this verse. We may not think being a coward is as serious as these other sins, but God takes it very seriously.

Cowardice tops the list of those who will suffer the **second death** in the lake of fire and brimstone.

Knowledge gives us **confidence**, and confidence is **power** against fear.

How to Overcome Fear

Since God has not given us a spirit of fear, it is obvious that we can overcome fear. God Himself is the means by which we can conquer our fears. "I sought the Lord, and He heard me, and delivered me from all my fears" (Ps. 34:4). Consider the following ways we can seek the Lord with regard to overcoming our fears.

1. **Learn to trust in God.** "The fear of man brings a snare, but whoever trusts in the Lord shall be safe" (Prov. 29:25). Trusting in the Lord is a solution to fear. Our faith has to grow to the point we believe we are under the watchful care of God (Luke 12:4-7). We are more valuable to God than many of us realize. He loves us and cares for us. He knows more about us and our needs than we do.

   "For you did not receive the spirit of bondage again to fear, but you received the Spirit of adoption by whom we cry out, 'Abba, Father'" (Rom. 8:15). Bondage to sin brings fear, but adoption as a child of God frees us from fear. We are under His divine care.

   Like Paul, we need to be able to say, "for I know whom I have believed and am persuaded that He is able to keep what I have committed to Him until that Day" (2 Tim. 1:12). Have we really learned to trust God?

2. **Learn to live in the presence of God.** When I was little, I was not afraid of anything as long as my Dad was around. He was bigger than any problem I could face. We cannot physically see God, but if we are truly walking by faith, we know God is always with us (Heb. 13:5-6). Such assurance should give us all the courage we need to serve Him without fear (Josh. 1:9).

   When the Syrians surrounded Elisha and his servant, the servant saw the enemy and cried out, "'Alas, my master! What shall we do?' Elisha answered, 'Do not fear, for those who are with us are more than those who are with them.' And Elisha prayed, and said, 'Lord, I pray, open his eyes that he may see.' Then the Lord opened the eyes of the young man, and he saw. And behold, the mountain was full of horses and chariots of fire all around Elisha" (2 Kings 6:15-17). Elisha was not afraid because he was aware of the spiritual realities that existed beyond his physical sight. His faith gave him confidence.

   "God is our refuge and strength, a very present help in trouble. Therefore we will not fear, even though the earth be removed, and though the mountains be carried into the midst of the sea" (Ps. 46:1-2). It does not matter what happens around us as long as God is with us. He is our refuge, strength, and a very present help.

3. Sanctify the Lord in our hearts.

> "And who is he who will harm you if you become followers of what is good? But even if you should suffer for righteousness' sake, you are blessed. 'And do not be afraid of their threats, nor be troubled.' But sanctify the Lord God in your hearts, and always be ready to give a defense to everyone who asks you a reason for the hope that is in you, with meekness and fear..." (1 Peter 3:13-15)

Instead of the threat of harm troubling us, we are to sanctify the Lord God in our hearts. The word "sanctify" means "to consecrate or set apart." The word "lord" means master. Focusing upon serving and pleasing our Master, we will not be troubled by the threats and fears caused by man. Instead of fear distracting and paralyzing us, our concern is serving and pleasing God.

4. Learn to use our spiritual armor.
Along with sanctifying the Lord, we are to be ready to give an answer for what we believe (1 Peter 3:15). Knowledge gives us confidence, and confidence is power against fear. Armed with a correct understanding of the truth, sufficient to defend our faith, we have nothing of which to be afraid.

Paul tells us to be strong in the power of the Lord and put on the whole armor of God that we may be able to stand against the wiles of the devil (Eph. 6:10-17). The armor of God protects us. The word of God ("sword of the Spirit") is our weapon. The more we learn about the word of God, the more familiar we become with it. The more we learn to use it, the less we have to fear.

Notice this armor provided by the Lord protects our front. We must face our fears in order to overcome them.

5. Pray.
After putting on the whole armor of God, we are to pray always with all prayer and supplication in the Spirit (Eph. 6:18). Prayer is essential to making this armor work.

There is great strength in prayer (Acts 4:29-31; Phil. 4:6-7; Ps. 55:4-5, 16-17, 22).

Conclusion

A problem with fear is not insignificant. It keeps one from pleasing God, serving Him, and going to heaven.

God has not given us a spirit of fear, but of power, love, and a sound mind. If we have a problem with fear, know God was not the one who put fear in our heart. Follow what the Bible says to overcome fear. Learn to trust in God, take courage in His promises, and focus on serving Him knowing He has already gained victory. Let us use our armor, and lean upon the Lord in prayer.

References

Guralnik, David B. *Webster's New World Dictionary of the American Language*. New York, NY: 1986.

Questions

1. In what two ways does the Bible use the word "fear?" _____
    _____
    _____

2. What is the difference between "fear" and "caution" or "concern?" _____
    _____
    _____

3. Can we be saved if we are afraid to confess Christ (Matt. 10:32-33; Rom. 10:9-10)? _____
    _____

4. Why did Joseph of Arimathea keep his faith a secret (John 19:38)? _____
    _____

5. Why did King Saul say he disobeyed the command of the Lord (1 Sam. 15:24)? _____
    _____
    _____

6. What happened to the servant who buried his master's talent (Matt. 25:25-30)? _____
    _____

7. What will happen to those who do not obey the gospel (2 Thess. 1:8-9)? _____
    _____

8. How can fear make one's life miserable? _____
    _____
    _____

9. Why did Gideon dismiss those men in his army who were fearful and afraid (Judges 7:2-3; Deut. 20:8)? _____
    _____

10. Who tops the list of those who will have their part in the lake of fire (Rev. 21:8)? _____
    _____
    _____

11. How does our trust in God do away with fear? _____
    _____
    _____

12. What does it mean to "sanctify the Lord God in our heart" (1 Pet. 3:15), and how does this help us overcome fear? _____
    _____
    _____

13. What has God given us to help us have courage (Eph. 6:10-17)?_____

_____

_____

14. How does prayer give us strength (Phil. 4:6-7; Ps. 55:22)? _____

_____

_____

Fill in the Blank

1. "Cast your _____ on the Lord, and He shall _____ you; He shall never _____ the _____ to be moved" (Ps. 55:22).

2. "I sought the Lord, and He _____ me, and _____ me from all my _____" (Ps. 34:4).

3. "And do not _____ those who kill the _____ but cannot kill the _____. But rather _____ Him who is able to destroy both soul and body in _____" (Matt. 10:28).

4. "However, no one spoke _____ of Him for _____ of the Jews" (John 7:13).

5. "Finally, my brethren, be _____ in the Lord and in the power of His might. Put on the _____ _____ of _____, that you may be able to _____ against the wiles of the _____" (Eph. 6:10-11).

6. "Be _____ for nothing, but in everything by _____ and _____, with thanksgiving, let your requests be made known to God; and the _____ ____ _____, which surpasses all _____, will _____ your hearts and minds through Christ Jesus" (Phil. 4:6-7).

7. "For God has not given us a spirit of _____, but of _____ and of _____ and of a _____ _____" (2 Tim. 1:7).

8. "So we may boldly say: 'The Lord is my _____; I will not _____. What can man do to me?" (Heb. 13:6).

PREJUDICE

The word "prejudice" is defined as: 1. a judgment or opinion formed before the facts are known; preconceived idea, favorable or, more usually, unfavorable. 2. a judgment or opinion held in disregard of facts that contradict it. 3. suspicion, intolerance, or irrational hatred of other races, creeds, regions, occupations, etc. (Guralnik).

A prejudiced person is one who has their mind made up without knowing all the facts and sometimes without caring to know all the facts. Prejudice is an exercise in willful ignorance and conceit resulting in wickedness, hatred, injustice, violence, and sometimes death. It is a violation of what our Lord offered as the second greatest commandment (Matt. 22:39) and what many people call the "Golden Rule" (Matt. 7:12). Such a thing should not be a part of a Christian's character. Sadly for some Christians, it is.

Prejudice is a violation of what many people call the "**Golden Rule.**"

Biblical Examples of Prejudice

Prejudice is a scar on the face of this nation that has yet to heal. However, prejudice is not a new thing. It has plagued mankind throughout history.

- The Egyptians were prejudiced against the Hebrews (Gen. 43:32).

- The Jews and Samaritans were prejudiced against each other (John 4:9). The Samaritan race was the result of Jews intermarrying with Gentiles. The Jews despised the Samaritans as "half-breeds," and the Samaritans returned this hatred and violence back upon the Jews.

- The Jews against Gentiles (Acts 10:28). The Jews viewed all Gentiles, regardless of their individual character, as unclean and unfit for association.

- The Pharisees against publicans (Luke 18:9-14). The publicans were Jews who collected taxes for the Romans. The Jews viewed them as traitors (because they collected taxes for the Romans) and thieves (because they commonly charged more for taxes and kept the surplus). Because of this, all publicans were viewed as sinners, regardless of their individual character or business practices.

- Nazareth (John 1:43-46). Nathanael scorned the idea the Messiah could come from a town like Nazareth, asking, "Can anything good come out of Nazareth?" Apparently the Jews held the town of Nazareth in such low esteem, Nathanael had already judged nothing good could ever come out of that town.

The Results of Prejudice

1. **Prejudice closes man's eyes to the truth.** Prejudiced by the One speaking, the scribes and Pharisees closed their eyes and ears to the truth (Matt. 13:14-15). Since Jesus had not been trained in their schools and did not keep their customs, they had already determined He could not possibly be the Messiah.

   Many people today are in religious error for the same reason. They do not want to change their minds, beliefs, or practices—regardless of what the Bible says. Sometimes even Christians exhibit prejudice against preachers, papers, or local churches based upon judgments they have made without getting all of the facts.

   The battle for lost souls is fought in the minds of men (2 Cor. 10:4-5). The gospel cannot enter a closed mind, and prejudice closes minds.

2. **Dishonesty.** Someone has said, "An honest man in error, when he learns the truth, will either stop his error or stop being honest." Some people resort to dishonesty to perpetuate their prejudice. The Jews understood Jesus claimed He would rise from the dead in three days (Matt. 27:63). Jesus did rise from the dead, but instead of repenting and accepting Him as the Messiah, the Jews gave the guards money and told them to lie and claim the disciples had come and stolen the body (Matt. 28:11-15). The Jews were not going to let factual evidence stop them from destroying Christ.

3. **Hypocrisy.** The New Testament reveals many Jewish Christians had a hard time accepting the Gentiles into the church. Even Peter, whom the Lord had used to open the door of the gospel to the Gentiles, later fell victim to this prejudice (Gal. 2:11-13). In Antioch, while away from his Jewish brethren, Peter treated his Gentile brethren one way, but when some came from Jerusalem, he withdrew himself from the Gentiles and treated them a different way. His influence even led others to play the hypocrite with him.

4. **Anger.** God called Jonah to be an instrument of mercy towards the people of Nineveh (Jonah 1:2). Jonah hated

> The **gospel** cannot enter a **closed mind**, and **prejudice** closes minds.

the people of Nineveh and wanted them to be destroyed. He despised the idea of helping them repent and fled in the opposite direction (v. 3). When he reluctantly went to Nineveh and preached to the people, they repented, and God spared their lives, but it angered Jonah and he wanted to die (4:1-2). Because of his prejudice, all Jonah "saw" in Nineveh were enemies, but God saw people whom He loved and wanted to spare.

Although Jonah did not personally do anything to harm the people of Nineveh, his reluctance to preach to them indicated he wanted to see them destroyed. Unfortunately, the anger aroused by prejudice often results in violence and death.

5. **Sin.** James wrote to Christians who were judging others by their appearance (James 2:1-9). They treated those who appeared to be rich in an honorable manner, while dismissing those who appeared to be poor. In doing so, they dishonored the poor man, sinned against him, and brought shame upon themselves.

How to Overcome Prejudice

As we have seen, prejudice is an ungodly attitude leading men to commit different kinds of sins. However, this attitude does not have to remain a part of our character. The following suggestions can help us overcome the sin of prejudice.

1. **Remember God is not prejudiced.** The Bible teaches God is not a respecter of persons (Rom. 2:11). One's nationality does not matter to God. He cares about an individual's faith and obedience (Acts 10:34-35), not the color of their skin. God wants all men to be saved and to come to a knowledge of the truth (1 Tim. 2:3-4).

2. **Remember the Gospel is not prejudiced.** The Lord commissioned the apostles to "make disciples of all the nations" (Matt. 28:19) by preaching the gospel to "every creature" (Mark 16:15-16). Heaven's invitation extends to "whosoever" (Rev. 22:17). Only an individual can judge himself to be unworthy of the gospel. He does so by rejecting the gospel (Acts 13:46).

3. **Remember the cross is not prejudiced.** Our Lord's death on the cross resulted in the reconciliation of two groups (Jews and Gentiles) prejudiced against each other, making them one (Eph. 2:14-16). There are no racial, economic, social, or gender distinctions in Christ, giving one an advantage over the other (Gal. 3:26-28). We cannot cling

Love demands we give others the benefit of the doubt and allow them to **prove themselves** to us, instead of **stereotyping** them and **prejudging** them.

to the cross and claim the salvation found there while harboring prejudice in our hearts towards others.

4. **Learn to love all men.** The second greatest commandment is that we love our neighbor as our self (Matt. 22:39). Love works no ill toward another. It demands we give others the benefit of the doubt and allow them to prove themselves to us, instead of stereotyping them and prejudging them. The "Golden Rule" will not allow us to be prejudiced against others (Matt. 7:12). It demands we treat people the way we want to be treated. We do not want to be stereotyped and prejudged. Since we want to be taken on our own merit, we must do the same for others.

5. **Learn to look upon the heart.** We need to learn to look upon people the way God does; look upon one's heart and not the color of his skin (1 Sam. 16:7). God does not take into account all the factors we use to prejudge others. God judges a man by his character, not by his color. To criticize the color of one's skin is to criticize God's handiwork.

6. **Insist on getting all the facts before forming judgments about others.** Remember prejudice is a judgment formed before getting all the facts or without regard to the facts. Contrary to popular belief, God allows us to make judgments about people. However, we must be careful and honest in forming these judgments. The Bible teaches facts must be supported by the testimony of at least two witnesses (Deut. 19:15; Matt. 18:6). It also teaches we must get both sides of a story before forming a judgment (Prov. 18:17).

7. **Allow ourselves to change our minds about people and things.** When Nathanael prejudicially dismissed Jesus because He was from Nazareth, Philip simply said, "Come and see" (John 1:46). The only way Nathanael was going to change his views was for him to see for himself. When he did, he changed his mind about the Lord (vv. 47-49). Prejudice is a sin caused by willful ignorance. We overcome it by taking the time to get the facts and responding honestly to those facts.

Conclusion

Prejudice is a sin contrary to the nature of God, the universal appeal of the gospel, the work of the cross, and the demands of love. It has no place in the heart and life of a Christian. We can use whatever excuse we want to try to justify our prejudices, but in our heart we know they are sinful and wrong. Instead, we must do what we can to overcome this sin, and pray to God for help in removing it from our heart.

References

Guralnik, David B. *Webster's New World Dictionary of the American Language.* New York, NY: 1986.

Questions

1. Why did the Pharisees treat all tax collectors as sinners? _____
    _____
    _____

2. How did Nathanael respond to the idea the Messiah had come from Nazareth? _____
    _____
    _____

3. How did the Jews show their dishonesty with regard to Christ's resurrection (Matt. 28:11-15)?
    _____
    _____

4. How did Peter play the hypocrite in Antioch (Gal. 2:11-13)? _____
    _____
    _____

5. What were some Christians doing by showing partiality to their wealthy visitors (James 2:9)?
    _____
    _____

6. What does God want for all men (1 Tim. 2:3-4)? _____
    _____
    _____

7. The apostles were to make disciples of _____ (Matt. 28:19).

8. How can love keep us from being prejudiced against others? _____
    _____
    _____

9. Man looks at the outward appearance, but God looks at the _____ (1 Sam. 16:7).

10. What should we do before we make a judgment against another person (Deut. 19:15;
    Prov. 18:17)? _____
    _____
    _____

11. Did Nathanael ever change his mind concerning Jesus (John 1:46-49)? _____
    _____

Thought Question

Why are some people prejudiced against the truth found in God's Word?

Fill in the Blank

1. "Therefore, whatever you want men to do to you, _____ _____ _____ _____, for this is the Law and the Prophets" (Matt. 7:12).

2. "And the second is like it: 'You shall love your _____ as _____'" (Matt. 22:39).

3. "My brethren, do not hold the _____ of our Lord Jesus Christ, the Lord of glory, with _____" (James 2:1).

4. "The first one to plead his cause seems _____, until his neighbor comes and _____ him" (Prov. 18:17).

5. "There is neither _____ nor _____, there is neither _____ nor _____, there is neither _____ nor _____; for you are all _____ in Christ Jesus" (Gal. 3:28).

6. "For there is no _____ with _____" (Rom. 2:11).

7. "But the Lord said to Samuel, 'Do not look at his _____ or at his physical stature, because I have refused him. For the Lord does not see as man sees; for man looks at the _____ _____, but the Lord looks at the _____'" (1 Sam. 16:7).

8. "And He said to them, 'Go into _____ the world and preach the gospel to _____ creature'" (Mark 16:15).

9. "And the Spirit and the bride say, 'Come!' And let him who hears say, 'Come!' And let him who thirsts come. _____ desires, let him take the water of life freely" (Rev. 22:17).

UNFORGIVING

There is a sin present in the lives of some Christians that angers God, grieves brethren, stifles the cause of Christ, and causes men to lose their eternal souls. It is the sin of refusing to forgive others.

Some brethren seemingly do not want to forgive those who have sinned against them. They prefer to nurse a grudge, honor their wounded pride, and cling to memories of past offenses than let these things go, mend broken friendships, and receive a penitent brother.

We Are Commanded to Forgive One Another

Forgiveness is not optional. We must forgive our brother from our heart. "And be kind to one another, tenderhearted, forgiving one another, even as God in Christ forgave you" (Eph. 4:32). To refuse to obey a command of the Lord is a sin.

It is important to forgive our brethren. According to Jesus, our forgiveness from God depends upon our willingness to forgive others.

> "For if you forgive men their trespasses, your heavenly Father will also forgive you. But if you do not forgive men their trespasses, neither will your Father forgive your trespasses" (Matt. 6:14-15).

> "And whenever you stand praying, if you have anything against anyone, forgive him, that your Father in heaven may also forgive you your trespasses. But if you do not forgive, neither will your Father in heaven forgive your trespasses" (Mark 11:25-26).

On one occasion, Peter questioned the Lord regarding the number of times he had to forgive his brother. "Lord, how often shall my brother sin against me, and I forgive him? Up to seven times?" (Matt. 18:21). Peter was being generous when he suggested the number seven. The rabbis of his day taught a man was to forgive three times, but never four.

The Lord replied, "I do not say to you, up to seven times, but up to seventy times seven" (v 22). When Jesus responded "seventy times seven" He was showing a disciple's willingness to forgive

Our **forgiveness** from God is **conditioned** upon our willingness to **forgive others**.

must be limitless. Peter was looking for the bare minimum, but Jesus taught we must be willing to forgive others as often as we want God to forgive us.

Jesus went on to speak a parable as a means of explaining this truth to Peter (vv 24-35). In the parable, a master forgave one of his servants an enormous debt he had no hope of ever repaying. This forgiven servant then went out and found a fellow servant who owed him a minuscule debt. He threw his fellow servant into prison and demanded the amount be repaid. When the master found out what had happened, he was angry and delivered the wicked servant to the torturers until the original debt was repaid.

As he rebuked the unforgiving servant, the master asked, "Should you not also have had compassion on your fellow servant, just as I had pity on you?" (v 33). Peter was looking for the minimum number of times he had to forgive. Jesus taught our willingness to forgive others must be comparable to God's willingness to forgive us. The Bible teaches God's mercy and willingness to forgive are great (Ps. 103:8-14; 1 John 1:9).

When Our Brother Repents

Jesus taught us to forgive our brother when he repents. "Take heed to yourselves. If your brother sins against you, rebuke him; and if he repents, forgive him. And if he sins against you seven times in a day, and seven times in a day returns to you, saying, 'I repent,' you shall forgive him" (Luke 17:3-4). To repent meant to turn or to change. There can be no forgiveness from God without repentance (Luke 13:3; Acts 8:22, 17:30).

When our brother sins against us, we are to rebuke him. If he will not listen to us, we are to take one or two more brethren with us and confront him again. If he will not listen to them, we are to tell the church, and he is to be disciplined (Matt. 18:15-17). However, if our brother repents, we are to forgive him.

It can be a great challenge to respond to our brother's repentance in a proper manner. This brother has wronged us and caused us pain, but now he has made things right. If we are not careful, our pride will find a way to keep us from reconciling with our brother. We will insist he feel more pain and show more sorrow. We will claim we need more restitution, more proof of sincerity, more time to heal, etc. However, the Bible does not tell us we have a right to hold off offering forgiveness until we feel like forgiving. We are to forgive when our brother repents.

In 2 Corinthians 2:6-11 the apostle Paul gave the follow-up instructions regarding a man who had his father's wife (1 Cor. 5). The Corinthians had administered the discipline, and it resulted

> "If we are **unwilling** to forgive until the humiliation, hurt or offense is **transferred back** to the offender, we really have **not forgiven**."
>
> –Butler, 384

in the man's repentance (v. 6). Now that the brother had repented, Paul instructed them to *forgive* him, *comfort* him, and *reaffirm their love* for him (vv. 7-8). Other Bible passages say nothing about a probationary period in which a penitent brother is to prove himself to the members. He is to be forgiven, accepted back into fellowship, and the matter is to be considered closed.

Responding to a brother's repentance provides a test for our faith. Will we be "obedient in all things" (v. 9) and receive him, or will we give in to pride and try to find a reason to refuse forgiveness? Refusing to forgive gives Satan an advantage (v. 11). He will use the opportunity to fill our heart with bitterness and fill our brother's heart with despair. In the end, we will lose our soul because we refused to forgive.

When There Is No Repentance

God desires that sins between brethren be resolved in a way that results in reconciliation. The relationship needs to be restored to a state of peace and harmony. This cannot be done unless the offender shows sincere repentance and the offended offers forgiveness from the heart. Where there is no repentance, there can be no reconciliation.

However, this does not mean the offended brother is best served by carrying a load of anger and resentment regarding the offense. "Actually, we must have a willingness to forgive even if our enemy does not repent. If he does not repent, our willingness to forgive will not profit him but it will certainly profit us" (Butler 384). While the sin cannot be forgiven and the relationship cannot be restored without repentance, the offended brother needs to learn to give up his resentment against the brother who has done him wrong. This pent up emotion will slowly poison his heart and life.

Hanging on the cross, Jesus prayed, "Father, forgive them, for they do not know what they do" (Luke 23:34). These individual sinners did not receive forgiveness until they came to a state of repentance regarding their involvement in the Lord's death, but the Lord Himself let the matter go. He died without anger and resentment in His heart regarding the ill treatment He received from sinners (1 Pet. 2:21-23). We must follow the Lord's example and learn to let go of offenses we have suffered.

How to Overcome the Sin of Unforgiveness

Those who struggle with an unforgiving spirit need to recognize this sin in their heart and strive to overcome it. The following

We must follow the **Lord's example** and learn to let go of **offenses** we have suffered.

suggestions will help one challenged by withholding forgiveness from a brother who repents.

1. **Take heed to ourselves.** When someone hurts us, we usually want to strike back in vengeance or shrink away to protect ourselves. Both reactions are natural, but neither reaction is in accordance with the teaching of our Lord. Thus, we must take heed to ourselves (Luke 17:3). Reason must override emotion. Satan will use the offense as a temptation for us to sin, but we must remember when someone sins against us, we do not have the right to sin in return. We must put hurt feelings and injured egos aside and fulfill our obligation in this matter.

2. **Do away with limits to our forgiveness.** While some people place limitations upon their willingness to forgive others, Jesus taught our willingness to forgive others must be without any limits (Luke 17:4; Matt. 18:21-22). When Jesus told Peter he must be willing to forgive "seventy times seven," He was not saying Peter was to keep a ledger and withhold forgiveness after the 490th offense. He was exaggerating Peter's original number (seven) to teach his willingness to forgive must be without any restrictions. How often must we forgive our brother? We must forgive as often as he repents.

3. **Value reconciliation and renewed fellowship over defending our injured pride.** There are some things more important than our feelings. "Behold, how good and how pleasant it is for brethren to dwell together in unity!" (Ps. 133:1). Sin destroys the unity shared between brethren, so repentance and forgiveness are necessary in order to restore this unity. With regard to restoring unity, withholding forgiveness is just as much an obstacle as refusing to repent.

Christians are to be known by their love for one another (John 13:35). When fighting, biting, and devouring one another (Gal. 5:14-15), we indicate to others our personal feelings are more important than the cause of Christ. It grieves Christians to see their brethren withhold forgiveness (Matt. 18:31). The only way we can walk worthy of the gospel of Christ is if we reconcile our differences, stand fast in one spirit, and strive together (not against one another) for the faith of the gospel (Phil. 1:27).

4. **Remember we stand in need of forgiveness.** Jesus taught us to pray, "And forgive us our debts, as we forgive our debtors" (Matt. 6:12). His teachings clearly link the forgiveness of our sins with our willingness to forgive others (Matt. 6:14-15; Mark 11:25-26).

When **fighting, biting, and devouring** one another, we indicate to others our **personal feelings** are more important than the **cause of Christ**.

In the parable of the unforgiving servant, the wicked servant refused to forgive a fellow servant after receiving forgiveness from an enormous debt by his master (Matt. 18:32-33). If God can forgive us when He has done nothing against us, upon what ground can we, as imperfect sinners, withhold forgiveness from a brother who repents? If we do not forgive, we will not be forgiven.

5. **Remember that sins committed against us do not compare to the sins we have committed against God.** The great contrast in debts (ten thousand talents vs. one hundred denarii – Matt. 18:24, 28) emphasizes the fact there is no comparison between the sins we have committed against the holy God and the wrongs we have personally suffered from our fellow man. If God is ready and willing to forgive us a debt we have no hope of repaying, how can we withhold the cancelation of a debt against us?

"How much do we owe the Lord? Some people do not feel that they owe Him anything. They breathe God's air, devour His sunshine and rainfall, yet never give Him a passing glance or one ounce in return. Other people acknowledge that they owe the Lord something, while others confess that they owe the Lord much. But this parable smacks at our vanity and self-reliance and says to each of us, 'You owe the Lord much more than you can ever pay'" (Lightfoot 61).

6. **Remember that receiving mercy obligates us to show mercy.** In the parable, the master said, "Should you not also have had compassion on your fellow servant, just as I had pity on you?" (Matt. 18:33). If God has forgiven us, He expects us to be willing to forgive our fellow man. There is no way we can pay back the debt of our sins against God, but the way God wants us to "repay" His mercy is to cancel out the debt of sins others have committed against us.

Paul taught Christians to forgive one another on the basis of Christ forgiving us. "Bearing with one another, and forgiving one another, if anyone has a complaint against another; even as Christ forgave you, so you also must do" (Col. 3:13).

7. **Remember God's blessings are given with the same measure we use upon others.** The Scriptures set forth this truth: "…with the measure you use, it will be measured back to you" (Matt. 7:2; cf. Luke 6:38). We cannot afford God to be stingy with His mercy and forgiveness towards us. If we have condemned others without mercy and pity, God will do the same thing to us (Matt. 18:33-35).

When we stand before the Lord in judgment, we will not care about the wrongs committed against us. We will not

When we stand before the Lord in **judgment**, we will not care about the **wrongs** committed **against us**.

have the opportunity to justify our resentment and refusal to forgive those who have hurt us. We will fall on our faces before the holy God and beg for His mercy and forgiveness. The only way we can expect to receive any mercy then is if we have shown mercy in our lives. "For judgment is without mercy to the one who has shown no mercy. Mercy triumphs over judgment" (James 2:13).

8. **Love others as we love ourselves.** The second greatest commandment is "You shall love your neighbor as yourself" (Matt. 22:39). Few things are more difficult than being denied forgiveness. When we have sinned against another, felt genuine remorse, repented, and sought to make things right, we do not want a door slammed in our face. If we would not want to be treated this way, we should not treat others like this (Matt. 7:12).

Conclusion

"The world's worst prison is the prison of an unforgiving heart. If we refuse to forgive others, then we are only imprisoning ourselves and causing our own torment. Some of the most miserable people I have met in my ministry have been people who would not forgive others. They lived only to imagine ways to punish these people who had wronged them. But they were really only punishing themselves" (Wiersbe 67).

Some of the most miserable Christians known are men and women who refuse to forgive and let things go. One brother in Christ could tell the month, day, and year of a wrong committed against him. He refused to forgive others. This is the extreme opposite of the Lord's teaching of "seventy times seven." The truth be told, many Christians lie somewhere between the Lord's teaching and this erring brother's extreme attitude. Unforgiving to any degree does not belong in the heart of a Christian. If we have a problem forgiving a brother, we need to overcome this sin.

References

Butler, Paul T. *The Gospel of Luke*. Joplin, MO: College Press Publishing Company, 1981. 384. Print.

Lightfoot, Neil R. *Lessons From the Parables*. Grand Rapids, MI: Baker Book House, 1965. 61. Print.

Wiersbe, Warren W. *The Bible Exposition Commentary*. 1. Colorado: Chariot Victor Publishing, 1989. 67. Print.

Questions

1. How important is our willingness to forgive our brother (Matt. 6:14-15; Mark 11:25-26)?
   _____
   _____

2. How many times did Peter offer to forgive his brother (Matt. 18:21)?_____
   _____

3. What did the Lord mean when He responded "seventy times seven" (v. 22)? _____
   _____
   _____

4. Describe God's willingness to forgive us from Psalm 103:8-14._____
   _____
   _____

5. What are we to do if our brother sins against us (Luke 17:3)? _____
   _____
   _____

6. What are we to do if he repents (Luke 17:3)? _____
   _____
   _____

7. What three things were the Corinthians told to do to the brother who had repented of his sin (2 Cor. 2:7-8)? _____
   _____
   _____

8. Sin destroys the relationship between brethren. What two things are necessary in order for this relationship to be restored?_____
   _____
   _____

9. What did Jesus pray as He was being crucified (Luke 23:34)? _____
   _____
   _____

10. Why did Jesus tell us to "take heed" to ourselves when a brother sins against us (Luke 17:3)?
    _____
    _____

11. How are disciples of Christ to be identified (John 13:35)? _____
    _____
    _____

12. How can our conduct be worthy of the gospel of Christ (Phil. 1:27)? _____
_____
_____

13. What was the purpose for the contrast of the debts in the parable of the unforgiving servant (Matt. 18:24, 28)?_____
_____
_____

14. What "measure" will God use when He shows us mercy and forgiveness (Matt. 7:2; Luke 6:38)? _____
_____
_____

15. What triumphs over judgment (James 2:13)?_____
_____
_____

Discussion Questions

1. How can we conclude an unforgiving attitude is a sin? _____
_____
_____

2. How does receiving mercy obligate us to show mercy to others? _____
_____
_____

3. What is the best way for us to handle a sin when the offending brother refuses to repent?
_____
_____

4. How does the second greatest command (Matt. 22:39) apply to our willingness to forgive?
_____
_____

5. How can we forgive someone who has caused us great pain and suffering? _____
_____
_____

INDIFFERENCE

The word "indifference" is not found in the Bible. However, several passages address the subject. While we may not appreciate or understand how something like indifference can be considered a sin, the Bible reveals it is a sin against both God and man.

The word "indifferent" means "1. having or showing no partiality, bias, or preference; neutral; 2. having or showing no interest, concern or feeling; uninterested, apathetic, or unmoved." The word "indifference" means "lack of concern, interest, or feeling; apathy" (Guralnik).

Indifference is disinterest, coldness, apathy, detachment, or unconcern. God seeks to find the opposite attitude in man. God calls us to make a decision and choose a side with regard to serving Him (Josh. 24:15; 1 Kings 18:21; Rev. 3:15). Jesus taught that men were either with Him or against Him (Matt. 12:30). There is no middle ground regarding our commitment to the Lord. When we consider what God has done for us, we must realize indifference is one of the most insulting attitudes that one can have towards God.

Indifference is a sin. Jesus told the Laodiceans to repent (Rev. 3:19). When was anyone ever told to repent when they had not sinned? Their indifference (the fact that they were neither cold nor hot) was resulting in a separation from Christ. He was ready to spew them out of His mouth (v 16). Sin separates us from God. Thus we must logically conclude indifference is a sin.

Indifference is a calloused disregard for the love of God and the plight of our fellow man. As such, it is unfitting in the life of a Christian. In this lesson, we will consider some of the consequences of indifference, as well as some things we can do to overcome this sin.

Consequences of Indifference

1. **It disgusts God.** The lukewarmness and indifference of the Laodiceans elicits a strong emotion out of the Lord—disgust (Rev. 3:16). Heartless indifference, not an overtly vile transgression, brings Jesus to the point of vomiting.

"Lukewarmness or indifference in religion is the **worst temper** in the world. If religion is a real thing, it is the **most excellent** thing, and therefore we should be in good earnest in it; if it is not a real thing, it is the **vilest imposture**, and we should be earnest against it. If religion is worth any thing, it is worth **every thing**; an indifference here is **inexcusable**."

–Matthew Henry, 914-915

"**Insensitivity** to the suffering of others, especially from society's most vulnerable, is **inexcusable**, and, although recompense might not arrive at all in this life, it is yet inevitable before a God who controls eternity.

Without **waiting** for somebody else— another person, the church, the government—to step in, the disciple of Christ will **step up** and come to the aid of the **poor, the widow, the orphan, the immigrant, the stranger**."

–Jeff Smith

2. **It discourages bretheren.** "As vinegar to the teeth and smoke to the eyes, so is the lazy man to those who send him" (Prov. 10:26). Those who are diligently striving to serve the Lord cannot help but be discouraged by those who profess the same Lord, but display indifference towards His cause. Things like poor attendance and contribution, lack of preparation for Bible classes, lack of interest in get-togethers, lack of concern for brethren who ask for prayers and help, preference for worldly interests, companions, standards, etc., are all sources of discouragement to faithful brethren.

3. **God's "house" is abandoned.** The prophet Haggai rebuked the Jews for rebuilding their own houses while neglecting their work on the Temple (Hag. 1:4-11). They suffered want because of the indifference they were showing towards the things of God.

God rebuked the shepherds for allowing His flock (Israel) to wander through the mountains with no one seeking or searching for them (Ezek. 34:1-10). These shepherds (spiritual leaders) only cared about themselves. They were indifferent to the spiritual well-being of those under their charge.

We can be just as indifferent towards the things of God's "house" today. The work of the church must be done. Elders, preachers, deacons, and Bible class teachers have important work to do. Souls will perish without hearing the gospel. Saints need to be taught, exhorted, strengthened, rebuked, and corrected. Sacrifices need to be made so this important work can be done.

4. **The needy are neglected.** There will always be poor individuals who are in need of help (Mark 14:7; James 1:27). There will always be urgent needs that must be met (Titus 3:14). Indifference causes us to turn a blind eye and deaf ear to the plight of those who are in desperate situations. Indifference also causes us to turn away from injustices and the plight of the helpless (Is. 57:1; Eccl. 4:1). David felt abandoned because he felt as if no one cared for his soul (Ps. 142:4).

5. **We will lose our soul.** The Bible makes it clear destruction and damnation are the ultimate consequences of man's indifference towards the things of God.

   • "Because they do not regard the works of the Lord, nor the operation of His hands, He shall destroy them and not build them up" (Ps. 28:5).

   • "He who keeps the commandment keeps his soul, but he who is careless of his ways will die" (Prov. 19:16).

- "And it shall come to pass at that time that I will search Jerusalem with lamps, and punish the men who are settled in complacency, who say in their heart, 'The Lord will not do good, nor will He do evil.' Therefore their goods shall become booty, and their houses a desolation; they shall build houses, but not inhabit them; they shall plant vineyards, but not drink their wine" (Zeph. 1:12-13).

We are to work out our salvation with fear and trembling (Phil. 2:12; Heb. 2:3). Carelessness and indifference will cause us to neglect this important work to the point we lose our soul's salvation.

How to Overcome Indifference

1. **Love.** Many people believe "hate" is the opposite of love, but it isn't. Indifference is the opposite of love. Love is a strong emotion, as is hate, but indifference is the absence of any emotion.

   What causes indifference in the marriage relationship? Perhaps one has lost the other's respect, one has failed to consider the needs and interests of the other, one has taken the other for granted, etc. Love keeps these things from happening.

   Love provokes us to do good for others (1 Cor. 13:4-7; 1 John 3:17-18). When we fail to do the positive things required to maintain a proper relationship, it will die. When we fail to do the positive things required to maintain a proper relationship with God (prayer, Bible study, worship, etc.) it will leave a void and a vacuum that Satan will fill.

2. **Zeal.** The Laodiceans were indifferent towards Christ. He told them to "be zealous and repent" (Rev. 3:19). To have zeal is to have warmth or feeling for something or something. The Laodiceans needed to be warmed up, stirred up, and woken up. They needed to become alive and active.

   The Bible tells us to serve the Lord with zeal (Rom. 12:11; Heb. 6:11-12). Zeal comes from the fellowship and association we have with our brethren (Heb. 10:24-25; 2 Cor. 9:2).

3. **Let Christ in our lives.** The reason the Laodiceans were lukewarm was because they had left Christ out of their lives (Rev. 3:20). The city of Laodicea was extremely wealthy. This gave the citizens a smug sense of self-sufficiency. "So wealthy was this city that its inhabitants declined to receive aid from the government after the place had been partly wrecked by an earthquake" (Hendriksen 76). Apparently, the church in Laodicea had the same attitude towards Christ.

Members who are **indifferent** about the Lord's church are likely those who have **invested the least** of themselves into it.

They had become complacent. They felt they were managing just fine on their own. This caused them to be indifferent towards the Lord's instructions and warnings.

Left alone, liquid will slowly work its way to room temperature. Something has to be added to it to make it warm or cold. The same is true with a Christian. If we separate ourselves from Christ, we will slowly take on the "temperature" of our surroundings, becoming indifferent to the commitment we have made to the gospel. If we let Christ back into our lives (through Bible study and faithful service), we will become hot again.

4. **Give of ourselves.** The Macedonians were not indifferent to the needs of the suffering saints. "For I bear witness that according to their ability, yes, and beyond their ability, they were freely willing, imploring us with much urgency that we would receive the gift and the fellowship of the ministering to the saints. And not only as we had hoped, but they first gave themselves to the Lord, and then to us by the will of God" (2 Cor. 8:3-5). They gave out of their poverty to help others because they "first gave themselves to the Lord."

We cannot help but be indifferent about something in which we have no interest. For instance, I am completely indifferent about the business section of the newspaper because I do not have anything invested in it. Once we invest ourselves (our time, energy, interest, etc.) in something, it means something to us. Members who are indifferent about the Lord's church are likely those who have invested the least of themselves into it. We are to give ourselves to the Lord, to the work of the local church, and to our brethren, not for personal gain or praise of men, but because it is right and good for us to do so.

5. **Pray.** Prayer is available to help us. If we see indifference is a problem in our heart, we can pray earnestly, and God will help us overcome it (Matt. 7:7-8).

Conclusion

God is not indifferent about our indifference. He calls us to make a choice. When we consider what God has done for us, how can we choose to be indifferent toward Him? Indifference can also be shown in a lack of love for our fellow man. It is a neglect for others born out of an undue focus upon our own opportunities, successes, and happiness.

Indifference can be overcome if we will practice love, pursue zeal, give of ourselves, and let Christ back into our life. A failure to do so will result in the loss of our souls, and we cannot afford to be indifferent about our souls (Matt. 16:26).

References

Guralnik, David B. *Webster's New World Dictionary of the American Language*. New York, NY: 1986.

Hendriksen, William. *More Than Conquerors*. Grand Rapids, MI: Baker Book House, 1985. 76. Print.

Henry, Matthew. *Matthew Henry's Commentary on the Whole Bible*. 6. Peabody, MA: Hendrickson Publishers, 1991. 76. Print.

Questions

1. Define indifference._____
    _____

2. What did Joshua and Elijah call upon the people to do (Josh. 24:15; 1 Kings 18:21)? _____
    _____

    _____

3. Jesus said, "He who is not with Me is _____ _____" (Matt. 12:30).

4. Why should we consider indifference to be a sin (Rev. 3:16-19)?_____
    _____

    _____

5. How is indifference an insult to God?_____
    _____

6. Describe how a Christian's indifference can be manifested._____
    _____

    _____

7. Why is a Christian's indifference a discouragement to his brethren? _____
    _____

    _____

8. Why were the Jews rebuked by the prophet Haggai (Hag. 1:4-11)? _____
    _____

    _____

9. Why was God's flock (Israel) "scattered over the whole face of the earth," and who was God
    holding responsible (Ezek. 34:1-10)?_____
    _____

    _____

10. How does indifference affect the work of the church? _____
    _____

    _____

11. What effect will indifference eventually have upon our soul? _____
    _____

    _____

12. How did the Laodiceans' self-sufficiency lead to their indifference (Rev. 3:17)?_____
    _____

    _____

13. Describe how the following things can help us overcome indifference:

Love _____

Zeal _____

Letting Christ in our lives _____

Giving of ourselves _____

Prayer_____

True or False

1. _____ Jesus said it was all right for men to remain undecided about Him (Matt. 12:30).

2. _____ Jesus would have preferred the Laodiceans to be cold over being lukewarm (Rev. 3:15).

3. _____ The Laodiceans were told to be zealous and to repent (Rev. 3:19).

4. _____ The Laodiceans had Christ at the center of their lives (Rev. 3:20).

5. _____ Love can be shown with just our words and intentions (1 John 3:18).

6. _____ David never felt abandoned by others (Ps. 142:4).

7. _____ Indifference has no serious effect upon the Lord's work.

8. _____ No real harm will come to those who are indifferent (Prov. 19:16).

9. _____ Zeal comes from disassociation with brethren.

10. _____ The Corinthians were generous because they first gave themselves to the Lord (2 Cor. 8:3-5).

CPSIA information can be obtained at www.ICGtesting.com
Printed in the USA
LVOW11s1715281013

358786LV00005B/6/P

9 780985 493875